The Covenanted Self

The Covenanted Self
Explorations in Law and Covenant

Walter Brueggemann

edited by Patrick D. Miller

Fortress Press

Minneapolis

Cover photo copyright © 1999 Photodisc, Inc.
Cover design: Craig Claeys
Interior design: Beth Wright

Library of Congress Cataloging-in-Publication Data

Brueggemann, Walter.
    The covenanted self : explorations in law and covenant / by Walter Brueggemann ; edited by Patrick D. Miller.
       p.   cm.
    Includes bibliographical references and index.
    ISBN 0-8006-3176-5 (alk. paper)
    1. Bible. O.T.—Theology.   I. Miller, Patrick D.   II. Title.
BS1192.5.B77 1999
230'.0411—dc21   99-30511
                                           CIP

Manufactured in the U.S.A.   AF-3176
03   02   01   00   2   3   4   5   6   7   8   9   10

Contents

Editor's Foreword

IT IS ONE THING TO BE PROLIFIC AND ANOTHER THING TO BE PROFOUND. Few of us in the theological enterprise accomplish both things as well as Walter Brueggemann. This, the fifth volume of his collected essays,[1] comes forth not long after the appearance of his *magnum opus, Theology of the Old Testament.* Together they provide two of the three modes of Brueggemann's theological communication: sharp provocative essays both academic and ecclesial, major works on biblical topics and biblical theology, and commentaries. In all of his work, Brueggemann is wedded to careful investigation of texts, using all the critical tools available in the scholarly study of Scripture. He is first and foremost an exegete, but there is nothing ordinary about that enterprise as he crafts it, nothing "academic" about it except the expertise that goes into his interpretive work. He exemplifies what most of us in biblical studies seek to do and to teach: a deep reading of texts that brings their meaning to the surface and articulates their significance and their claims. What one hears seems to be both thoroughly there in the text and thoroughly confrontive of human existence. Even the most academic of his essays, those that appear in what we are accustomed to call "field journals," open up the text so that the reader is drawn into a sense of it as Scripture, as making claims and eliciting responses. This does not mean that no one disagrees with his results. That goes without saying, especially when the interpretation is as constantly challenging and demanding as Brueggemann's. But few go away unaffected by what they have read or heard.

One of the features of Brueggemann's work that is evident in a number of the essays in this volume is his continuing engagement with currents of contemporary life and thought. He is willing to risk the accusation of faddism in order to be sure that the resonance of Scripture with those currents is uncovered and articulated. Some of these modes of thought have engaged him over a long period of time. Thus one will find in these essays, as in others written some time ago, a conversation with object relations theory and indications that that theory about how relationship and the capacity for relationship develops in the growth of the human has much in common with insights from Scripture. When an Old Testament theologian places D. W. Winnicott in a conversation with Moses and the Apostle Paul, as Brueggemann does in an informal way in the first two essays in this volume, the horizons of the reader are significantly stretched and the wholeness of truth and knowledge is attested in unexpected ways. One does not expect a biblical theologian to know or care about such matters, but Brueggemann has never sought to fit into any particular mold or dominant expectation. Going his own way, all the time fully aware of and engaged with what others are doing, he ends up drawing many people, including many professional colleagues, along with him. At his most provocative, he cannot be ignored.

The essays in this volume come from the most recent period of Brueggemann's activity as a biblical interpreter. They reflect many familiar themes in his work but brought to bear here on new issues. It is no accident that this Reformed theologian places great weight upon *covenant* as the ancient and contemporary context in which obedience to the Lord of the universe is defined and expected. At least three components of his working with that theme are indicative of the way Brueggemann goes about the task of biblical interpretation and communication. One is his interest in *relating the biblical understanding of covenant,* a highly communal notion, to *theories of personality* that might be seen more individualistically but in this instance provide helpful analogies for clarifying the way the Bible relates the self to others (see, for example, "'Othering' with Grace and Courage" and "The Daily Voice of Faith").

A second major focus of Brueggemann's development of covenantal obedience is the *commandments*. Two of the essays here offer an interpretation of the Great Commandment (both parts), but they are hardly typical of the readings of these commandments in the commentaries. Indeed these essays, "The Cunning Little Secret of Certitude" and "Neighborliness and the Limits of Power in God's Realm," demonstrate one of the characteristic features of Brueggemann's interpretation: the *juxtaposition of texts in unexpected ways.* No treatment of any particular text is ever confined to speaking about that text alone, and the other texts that Brueggemann places in conversation with his primary focus are often surprising and even startling. Thus his treatment of the first part of the Commandment—to love the Lord with all that one has and is—not only draws in typical Great Commandment texts but puts primary weight on two psalms, Psalms 73 and 139, not usually thought of in this connection. But that is because Brueggemann has the capacity to see dimensions of the issue posed by the text that others may miss, and resonances—harmonious and discordant—among texts that seem to belong in different concert halls.[2] The musical image is quite appropriate, for Brueggemann creates chords, themes, melodies, and codas in an artistic fashion but as disciplined as the finest composer.

A third aspect of Brueggemann's broad-ranging exploration of covenant and commandment is the way in which that framework touches on *unexpected but significant dimensions of human existence*. His interpretation of the covenantal obedience embodied in the commandments as the joining of duty and desire is worked out specifically in relation to the spheres of *sexuality* and *economics* ("Duty as Delight and Desire"). The very heuristic treatment of the ninth commandment points to *euphemism, advertising,* and *propaganda* as primary examples of oppressive false witness against the neighbor and identifies *theological truth-telling* as the positive demand of the commandment ("Truth-Telling as Subversive Obedience"). The absolute devotion to God enjoined upon us by the First Commandment and the Great Commandment is seen as a challenge to various kinds of *certitude*. The Decalogue is a charter for the holiness of God and justice to the neighbor. Covenant obedience is a matter of *place* and thus Israel's vision of social reality is in terms of *land* ("Placed Between Promise and Covenant"), a theme Brueggemann has addressed in a full monograph and one that is indicative of his sense of the materiality of the divine promise and the concreteness of the realm in which good neighborliness is worked out.[3] That materiality is also the realm of blessing in the very specific and necessary reality of *food*. Brueggemann's history of food in the Bible is not the typical sort of word or thematic study. It asks about coveting, scarcity, sharing, and abundance, all in relation to food and the question of what is "enough for us" ("The Truth of Abundance: Relearning *Dayenu*"). In this essay and throughout, notice also some reflection on *anxiety* and what the Bible has to say about that to an age that can describe itself by such a term.

Finally, there are two larger matters to note as one reads these essays— and any of the rest of Brueggemann's work. One is that the reality of God stalks his work. No contemporary writer is more critical of the deity or more in awe of God than Walter Brueggemann. He knows this God only through the pages of Scripture and it is the Lord of Israel who provokes, frustrates, terrifies, and sustains him. His attraction to the "Jewishness" of the Old Testament is not so much to claim Jewish-Christian common ground —though he believes that common ground is large—as it is his sense that Jewish obedience does not preclude argument with the Holy One. His insistence on using the proper name "Yahweh" is a way of confronting himself and all the rest of us with the one whose ways and words are known in Scripture. That God, Brueggemann tell us, will be all over us and all around us. And that is both bad news and good.

Second, this contemporary prophet is haunted by the possibility of a world that is both more human and filled with the glory of God. His essays are partial but powerful efforts to define the kingdom of God, to help us see what a good neighborhood is like in hopes that we will want to create such a place and live there. It is such a neighborhood that the law of the Old Testament sought to define and the prophets to envision. He follows in their train.

Patrick D. Miller

Preface

THE REISSUE OF ALREADY PUBLISHED ARTICLES (ALL BUT ONE) IS AN ACT of some courage, for it assumes that things published in more obscure places will be of interest to a wider readership. I commit such an act of courage, because the four volumes of a like kind published heretofore by Fortress Press have received enough attention to add a fifth volume.

Because these several papers have been prepared for and presented on a variety of occasions, some of the marks of the initial local context are inescapable. For the same reason it is inevitable that there is some repetition and restatement of some of the same points, albeit in different contexts.

My specific thanks in connection to this volume are to three persons. Patrick D. Miller has again given me his wise counsel and his editorial judgment in the shaping of the volume, and I am again indebted to him for his generous investment in my work. Tempie Alexander has done her usual, (and each time immensely appreciated) work on the manuscript through countless recensions. Tim Simpson has worked in the detail of preparing the manuscript and the indices. To all three my hearty and abiding thanks. and my appreciation to Henry French and his colleagues at Fortress Press for again taking on such a project.

Walter Brueggemann
Fifth Sunday after Pentecost, 1998

1

"Othering" with Grace and Courage

FOR ALL THE VAGARIES OF OLD TESTAMENT SCHOLARSHIP, "COVENANT" looms large in ancient Israel, and in the faith of the church. For all of our study, we still have to determine how covenant is to be understood as a theological commitment, and how it is to be enacted as a mode of shared life. I understand covenant in our own time and place to be a radical alternative to consumer autonomy, which is the governing ideology of our society and which invades the life of the church in debilitating ways.

I will divide my comments into five parts, two that are foundational and three that seek to exposit on the basis of that foundation. The structure and development of my argument will be quite transparent.

1

I take the liberty of using the work "other" as a verb, for I mean to suggest that "other" is not simply a counter-object, but it is the risky, demanding, dynamic process of relating to one who is not us, one to whom we are accountable, who commands us, and from whom we receive our very life.

Hans Urs von Balthasar, that great Roman Catholic theologian, has written that in the year 1918 and the following year "one of the strangest phenomena of 'acausal contemporaneity' in the history of the intellect took place."[1] In that year, four scholars, apparently independent of each other, published on "the dialogical principle," which we know most popularly as the principle of "I-Thou." In addition to the work of Martin Buber, this included Franz Rosenzweig, Ferdinand Ebner, and Gabriel Marcel. To these names, moreover, we should add Eugen Rosenstock-Huessey. This bursting disclosure made clear that the human self is not an independent, autonomous agent but is always and necessarily preceded by a Thou, one radically other than us, who evokes, summons, authorizes, and "faiths" us into existence as persons. This "other" is endlessly inscrutable mystery and endlessly problematic to us, for we can neither escape from that other, nor are we able to seduce, capture, or possess that other who always stands free from and over against us. This quintessentially Jewish notion of reality, while mediated most powerfully by Buber, has more recently been important to the work of Emmanuel Levinas, and in a very different way to the argument of George Steiner concerning great literature.[2]

The definitional insight of this mode of thinking, which we may term "the dialogical principle" or "the principle of alterity," is that this restless, unsettleable relation is the irreducible core of what it means to be human. It is immediately evident that this dialogical principle is opposed to our usual, conventional understanding, both of ancient Hellenistic and of the modern Cartesian modes of reality. The ongoing process of life is to come to terms with this other who will practice *mutuality* with us, but who at the same time stands in an *incommensurate* relation to us. It is the tension of *mutuality* and *incommensurability* that is the driving force of a biblical notion of life.

Hebrews, Israelites, and Jews have known something odd and peculiar about this agent and subject of otherness. Abraham and Sarah at the outset find themselves addressed by a voice other than their own, who speaks to them a life-disrupting command and a life-energizing promise (Gen. 12:1-3). Moses and his community stand in terror at the mountain before this other who speaks to them ten uncompromising demands (Exod. 19:10-25, 20:1-17, 18-21), except that it is this same uncompromising God before whom they eat and drink and upon whom they "gaze" (Exod. 24:9-11).

In the wake of Abraham, Sarah, and Moses, moreover, the psalmists are stricken with the awfulness of the inescapable presence of this other:

> Where can I go from your spirit?
> > Or where can I flee from your presence?
> If I ascend to heaven, you are there;
> > if I make my bed in Sheol, you are there.
> If I take the wings of the morning
> > and settle at the farthest limits of the sea,
> even there your hand shall lead me,
> > and your right hand shall hold me fast.
> If I say, "Surely the darkness shall cover me,
> > and the light around me become night,"
> even the darkness is not dark to you;
> > the night is as bright as the day,
> > for darkness is as light to you.
> > > (Ps. 139:7-12, cf. Amos 9:2-4)

I suggest that "spirituality" is the enterprise of coming to terms with this other in a way that is neither excessively submissive nor excessively resistant. Such coming to terms is obviously no small matter. For this other is an endless threat to our safety and our integrity. This Thou always undermines whom we have chosen to be. The presence of the other always reminds us that we are addressed, unsettled, unfinished, underway, not fully whom we intend or pretend to be. For that reason, so much of life consists in fending off this life-threatening, life-giving otherness, for the other evokes in us terrible fears—phobias, we call them. And because this other must be fended off, we have our several strategies for fending off, which may take sociopolitical form or theological-moral-liturgic form. After all our phobias are in place and made to seem legitimate, however, this terrible Jewish reality pushes against us, and our conventional settlements of reality are subverted.

This troubled state, so our Jewish tradition bears witness to us, is a common reality for all and for each of us. But we are nonetheless the ones who have a name for this healing threat, who are baptized into this destiny of "othering," and who are pledged to give our life over to that process of othering. This work of othering is inescapable because this process of interaction is the awesome truth of our life. And any who seek to escape this troublesomeness, either in arrogance or in abdication, have not yet faced the terrible inconvenience that constitutes our very existence.

II

This "otherness," as Jews have always known, concerns the largeness and inscrutability of transcendence, which is why religious mystery will not go away. That is, the slippage of life has to do with the holiness of God. Our primal experience of otherness, however, is not in large transcendence but in the intimacy of very early childhood. So my second point is a big move from the alterity of Buber and Levinas to a reflection upon Object Relations theory, a theory of personality that I judge to be peculiarly congenial to scriptural notions of alterity, that is, to the demanding reality of covenant. D. W. Winnicott, a British pediatric psychiatrist, observed in his practice a long stream of mothers with young babies.[3] Out of his practical experience and observation, he fashioned a theory of ego formation.

Winnicott was deeply grounded in Freud, except that Freud had concluded that the decisive factors in personality were intrapsychic, that is, taking place inside the human person. Winnicott departed from Freud in a definitive way by insisting that the important issues in personality and in personality formation are interpersonal, that is, genuinely relational toward a real other who is an identifiable, reliable object, and not merely a subjective projection. That is, the definitional issue for the formation of the child is the baby's relation to mother. It is mother who constitutes the other, and *mutatis mutandis*, for our purposes, I suggest it is covenanting with mother that constitutes the first work of the child.

Now that relation with mother, as we all know, is tricky and demanding. Winnicott observed that while there are no perfect mothers, there are intuitively "good enough mothers," Winnicott's now classic term for the mother who knows intuitively to what must be done for the sake of the child.[4] And what must be done in the very earliest days of the baby's life is that the child must have an experience of omnipotence vis-à-vis the mother, must have the certitude that the mother exists fully and solely for the sake of the child and is attentive to every need and wish and desire of the baby. The mother acts out this devotion to the child by being fully attentive to and celebrating everything the baby does, from smile to burp to fart, and in so doing, helps the child gain a sense of self, of being fully valorized as she must be by this "thou" who gives the gift of self.

This sense of omnipotence in a healthy relation with the "mother-object" must be fully developed and must be in due season appropriately frustrated, lest the child become limitlessly self-indulgent. It is important, however, that the frustration of the child not be enacted until after the omnipotence has been fully experienced. The process of frustration occurs as the mother begins to distance herself from the child, so that the child notices that mother does not exist solely "for me" but has a life of her own. At the same time, in a healthy process the child acquires a sufficient self to notice that she can be a full self without the constant valorization of the mother, and the process of differentiation can advance.

Conversely, Winnicott also noticed what happens when the mother is not "good enough," that is, when the mother is not able to give herself over fully to the child, because she is distracted or excessively preoccupied with herself. As a consequence, the child is not valorized and does not develop a healthy sense of self, first valorized by and then differentiated from the other. Rather, such a child continues to seek valorization from the mother who cannot give it, seeks it even more desperately and cunningly. Very quickly, says Winnicott, the child learns that she cannot receive celebration and affirmation from the mother for the intrinsic act of being itself, for example, smiling, burping, or farting. Rather, the baby must turn from the self (which now does not work) to the moods and inclinations of the mother in order to please mother at all costs, even if the pleasing of mother is fraudulent. As a result, the baby must act against what she in fact wants, intends, needs, or feels. The outcome is a "false self," a phony self in which all sense of the real self is ceded over to mother, and the baby never receives or embraces or enacts a full, true self, but is devoted to mother in a life of bribery.[5]

Now this excursus into Object Relations theory pertains to our theme of covenanting, or as I have termed it "othering," in that in a healthy relation, as the baby is appropriately omnipotent and then frustrated, the baby develops the skills and sensitivity both *to hold advantage over mother* and *to yield appropriately to mother*, doing each as is germane to the moment. This dual capacity *to assert* and *to yield* is a remarkable skill that takes delicate and hard work, but it is what a healthy relation is all about. The failure to achieve this dual competence in "othering" leads either to a life of conformity (which Christopher Bollas terms "normotic personality") or to a life of arrogant self-indulgence that is never able to yield.[6] Or it leads to a duality in which there is an odd juxtaposition of conformity in some zones of life and self-indulgence in other zones of life, but never the delicate othering that produces health and constancy in relation to a real "other." (In our society the dominant ideology seeks to arrange matters for *conformity in sexuality* and *self-indulgence in consumer economics*.) But of course such lines of distinction cannot be sustained, and we begin to get a strange mix of conformity and self-indulgence, neither of which is appropriate to serious othering.

Now I trouble you with this model of otherness in personality theory for three reasons:

1. The struggle of a baby to learn the art of othering is difficult and crucial. It is an art that all of us sooner or later seek to learn. It belongs to our humanness to learn the art, because as these great Jewish thinkers have understood so well, our "I" depends upon this endlessly unsettling "Thou." One can see the riskiness of this two-fold act of asserting and yielding when a child in the same instant is both angry with mother, so angry that he wants to assault her, and yet desperately yearns to be embraced by her.[7] He wants omnipotence over her, and yet wills to cede his life over to her in order to be safe and to be affirmed. This tricky relation is, as any of us can attest, one that admits of no final closure or settlement, but is the endless work of humanness.

2. I suggest that "othering" with God and with neighbor is derivative from and informed by this primal othering with mother. I do not want to go all the way with Ava-Maria Rizzuto in saying that in our relation with parent we get our sense of relation to God, for in the end such a view is theologically reductionist.[8] Nonetheless, I also believe there is a good deal in it, and if the othering skills are thwarted with mother, one will have a very difficult time in relation to God and to neighbor. Thus if with mother a false self learns to fake it, I suspect this prepares the way for excessive submissiveness to God in which omnipotence vis-à-vis God comes to feel like blasphemy, because mother may not like it. Or conversely, if the child never learns to submit to mother in trust and confidence but has an unmitigated sense of autonomy, the outcome may be a graceless religion of self-sufficiency in which nothing is ever yielded and nothing is ever received.

The psalmist never confuses the parental relation with one's relation to God. But the psalmist also knows about this delicate and definitive relation between parental intimacy and God's transcendent fidelity:

> Yet it was you who took me from the womb;
> > you kept me safe on my mother's breast.
> On you I was cast from my birth,
> > and since my mother bore me you have been my God.
> Do not be far from me,
> > for trouble is near
> > and there is no one to help. (Ps. 22:9-11)
> If my father and mother forsake me,
> > the Lord will take me up. (Ps. 27:10)

In the first of these psalms, the affirmation about God who kept me safe on mother's breast is made in a self-asserting complaint. As you know, Psalm 22 begins in a protest about God's absence, and the great trust of the verses I have quoted is offset by the protest at the beginning. In the second psalm, the assertion of profound confidence in God is made in a self-surrendering song of trust, but only as the speaker contemplates abandonment by mother and father. Thus trust in Yahweh is linked to the relation of intimacy with parents that has failed.

3. I linger over this matter of the correlation between othering with God and othering with mother because I believe there is here a crucial learning in relation to covenant. I propose that unless one has learned to other well with mother in graceful and courageous ways, grace to surrender and courage to assert, one will not other well with God. Moreover, I propose that much of the struggle just now in the church (as in the larger society) is the result of folk who have not learned to other well, and who therefore other in excessive conformity or in excessive self-preoccupation—either way, operating as false selves. This causes the church to use excessive amounts of its energy on false issues. And because in such false selfhood the other (mother or God) is excessively demanding or excessively indulgent, transactions with the other are never liberated, healthy, or evangelical. There are various strategies for fending off the other, either God or neighbor, by doctrine, liturgy, morality, and piety. But these strategies do not produce missional energy. We must return, therefore, both theologically and emotionally-liturgically, to the most elemental intimacies wherein we may glimpse the shapes of transcendent fidelity. If it turns out that mother or father abandon, in demand or in indulgence, we wait yet to be taken up by this God who can complete the unfinished work of valorizing us as genuine selves.

III

Now with these foundational reflections upon *covenanting with transcendence* and *covenanting with intimacy*, I want to consider with you three zones of covenanting by way of expositing a relation to the other who gives us life.

First and most importantly, of course, our task (like that of ancient Israel) is to come to terms with the covenantal faithfulness of Yahweh who engages in *mutuality* with God's people, but who is never *commensurate* with that people. It is clear, if we consider Israel's normative text seriously, that the God of this people is not the God of scholastic theology, that is, not omnipotent, omniscient, or omnipresent. Equally clear, this God is not the warm fuzzy of therapeutic consumerism. Rather this God is an endlessly live, demanding, giving, surprising, problematic other in Israel's life. And Israel's life consists in coming to terms with this other who refuses to be slotted, in the strange transaction of mutuality and incommensurability.

My simple observation is that Israel learned to relate to this God of threat and gift by the sustained, delicate practice of *praise and complaint*. That is, the Psalter is the laboratory in which Israel works out its dangerous, inscrutable life with this most significant other, the Thou upon whom our life depends. This God, as Israel witnesses, is indeed "wholly other," but not in the one-dimensional way as some belated Barthians claim. The otherness of the God for Israel is like the otherness of mother, who valorizes in self-giving, self-forgetting ways, and who in holiness has God's own life to live, completely without regard for Israel.[9] This God must be praised, and Israel's covenanting activity, already undertaken by Miriam and her sisters in Exod. 15:20-21, is to learn in lyrical, doxological, self-abandoning ways to cede life over to God in complete surrender, trust, confidence, and joy. This God will be praised, exalted, magnified, blessed, and Israel's true vocation is indeed to get its mind off itself and "glorify God and enjoy God forever."

In their reflection upon creation, liberation, homecoming, and resurrection, the people of God cannot restrain themselves. Praise must be uttered, even though it is an act at least pre-rational if not irrational. Praise invites a poetic act of imagination about God and God's world. Covenanting means self-abandonment, giving self up for the other, and requires the healthy capacity to move beyond self-concern to the unutterable graciousness and awesomeness of God. Israel's Psalter ends in Psalm 150 with a lyrical outburst that is almost contentless in its exuberance. This correlates with Winnicott's notion that the child is able to recognize that mother has a life of her own that is to be affirmed and celebrated.

Winnicott, of course, knew that a healthy child does not and cannot begin in such an affirmation of mother's life but must first pay attention to his own life, his safety, his own joy and worth, and can think of little else until that is seriously established. In parallel fashion, Israel's Psalter does not begin with such self-abandoning praise.[10] It only culminates in such doxology after a long collection of harsh, demanding, insistent complaints and laments. Israel's first address to the covenanting God is one of self-insistence that means to draw Yahweh's attention and energy to Israel's plight. This is evident in Exod. 2:23-25 where the normative liberation of Israel begins when they "groaned . . . and cried out," and in response, *only in response*, God heard and acted. In like manner, the early part of Israel's Psalter is dominated by complaints, by acts of self-assertion that insist either that God has failed and now must act, or that the enemies are strong and God must now intervene in fidelity. Either way, the complaint is all about *us* and *our need* and *our insistence*.

Thus I read the Psalter as a dialectic of *self-assertion* in complaint and *self-abandonment* in praise, just as the child must first claim self and only then notice mother. I have no doubt that theologically and emotionally, self-assertion precedes self-abandonment, for there is no self to abandon or to pledge loyalty unless that self has been claimed and valorized. This means that the beginning of covenanting as a practical act of self-insistence is more abrasive than much deferential theology, and much more serious than much conventional self-indulgence. It is through urgent insistence that God can be bonded to my issues, so that I may be bonded to God's expectations.[11]

Thus I suggest that covenanting (and spirituality) consists in learning the skills and sensitivities that include both the courage to assert self and the grace to abandon self to another. Such covenanting recognizes that both parties have claims to make, and that one must learn the right time in which to pursue and honor each claim, and then have the confident, unencumbered freedom to move in both directions. My sense about much of theological education is that we tend to be either piously deferential or brazenly self-preoccupied, but neither alone leads to a "true self" nor to a faithful covenant.

IV

The second zone in which we are compelled to think about covenanting, that is, the practice of othering, is that of the neighbor. Of course the neighbor as other is even more problematic than God as other, because the neighbor is so near, so visible, and so daily. And clearly, we draw close to the problematic of otherness in theological education, for life in a seminary community, like life in any community, confronts us with all the challenges of neighborliness.

It is a truism that charity begins at home. It is, however, an equal truism that familiarity breeds contempt, that those closest to us can be intensely problematic for us. And if that were not tough enough, Jesus has widened the horizon of neighborliness to include stranger, alien, foreigner, and even enemy. Neighborliness is difficult in any case, but then we must introduce into the calculus the reality of power relations between the stronger and the weaker. That neighborliness touches as large an arena of life as the so-called developed economies of the last superpower, as well as the so-called underdeveloped societies, or we may say debtor economies. It touches such problematic issues as how the conventionally stronger male and the conventionally weaker female are to relate and the socially-determined stronger White and the socially-determined weaker Black are to relate. It touches the unnerving issue of neighbors who have rather different "preferences" or "orientations" about sexuality (depending upon how one chooses to articulate the matter). And into the mix of the schoolhouse is stirred the differential of grader and gradee, or administrator and non-tenured folk, and so forth, and we prefer in theological education to speak of "community" as though we have all things in common. I imagine any Christian community, certainly including a Christian academic community, has as its core work the gracious, courageous practice of othering, in the face of conventional forms of power relations that deny and preclude serious othering.

It is my suspicion that if we have not learned healthy othering in the intimacy of mothering, and if we have not learned the daring of othering with God's transcendent fidelity, then we are bound in our neighboring to miss out on much of the othering that belongs properly to the gospel. Indeed, around the matter of neighbors, our clumsiness and fearfulness often lead us to avoid others who are unlike us, to whom we do not want to give gifts, and from whom we do not intend to receive gifts, and under whose command we do not want to live. We organize our several phobias, resentments, and ambitions in order to be mainly with others who are not very otherly and so constitute no threat of otherness. Indeed, in some seminary communities, groups have been known to form in order to fence out certain neighbors who do not pray right or believe right or live right, and such a passion for purity works powerfully against neighborliness. It is, however, my judgment that we have no human neighbors who are as unlike us as this othering God is unlike us, and if in complaint and praise, in assertion and abandonment, we are genuinely at risk and in faith with this God, we shall find great resources of grace and courage for living with the neighbor, even the neighbor who is blatantly other.

Under this rubric I simply remind you of three phrases about neighbors, two from Paul and one from Deutero-Paul, because Paul and his tradition seem to have thought the most about the unending horizontal challenging of church life.

1. "If one member suffers, all suffer together with it; if one member is honored, all rejoice together with it" (1 Cor. 12:26). As you know, in 1 Cor. 12 Paul has just completed his eucharistic chapter 11 on the new covenant (11:25), and has considered the problem of pluralism under the rubric of "varieties of gifts, but the same Spirit" (12:4). He is on his way to the *agape* manifesto of chapter 13. In the midst of all this daring theological affirmation, Paul here talks about the church as a body with many members. And he has just written in 12:24-25,

> But God has so arranged the body, giving the greater honor to the inferior member, that there may be no dissension within the body, but the members may have the same care for one another.

Paul's subject is membership, all belonging to the same thing, being members of each other. But notice, it is not as though there is a body, and then you sign on as a member to an already existing body. No, "members of each other." Analogue: In a U.S. college, one works for a college or goes to college. But in Cambridge, the faculty is the college. You don't join the body; you are the body. It is not something already there, but how its members live shapes the quality, character, and future of the body.

This membership in and with and by and for each other has important distinctions between the more honored and the less honored. But here the inferior member is more honored—something about "the first and the last." In the seminary where I live, we have "Honors Day," and we always honor the superior members. But Paul thinks otherwise. Perhaps we should have an Honors Day for the less honorable.

Moreover, Paul envisions that members are bound together at the extremities of life, at the strong seasons of joy and sorrow where we live anyway, at those times when we are being exiled and brought home, crucified and raised to new life. But then, that is how and where most of us live each day. On our alert days, we ponder our unresolved losses and our treasured gains that are remembered or anticipated. It is this work of "joy and sorrow" that makes us timeful creatures, and not just effective, present tense automatons. Jesus is like that in his contacts with people. He works mostly at the extremities of peoples' lives, or by his presence he articulates and creates extremities where they thought none existed. Paul believes that an effective othering agent can indeed turn loose of his own sorrows and joys enough to attend to others, because in mothering intimacy and in holy transcendence we have had our own career of "joy and sorrow" fully valorized.

2. In the same letter, Paul writes twice,

> "All things are lawful," but not all things are beneficial. (1 Cor. 6:12, 10:23a)

And in the second version he adds the parallel,

> "All things are lawful," but not all things build up. (10:23b)

In the first of these passages, Paul is concerned with the abuse of the body, apparently in self-indulgence. In the second Paul addresses the vexed issue of illicit food. And while Paul champions great freedom, seeming to agree in principle with his Corinthian opponents, his pastoral sense of the well-being of the community overrides such freedom. He counsels the church to attend to the conscience of the more scrupulous members of the community.

Paul's aphorism is related to neighborliness and "othering" in the community. The church, or the church seminary, is not and should not be a community of many rules. On the "liberty of the Christian person," Paul is largely without scruples.[12] At least here, "Be free in the gospel." The problem of course is that such freedom taken by itself characteristically works to the advantage of the stronger party, and if in the exercise of such freedom somebody else gets hurt, that's tough.

Except that Paul's pastoral sensitivity curbs such gospel-given freedom. The curb is the conscience of the other member. Or more covenantally, the curb is the well-being of the community, before which the liberated and strong must yield to the membership, a membership that defines even the strong and the liberated. Thus the reality of the community comes before any liberty, and certainly before the liberty of any autonomous individual.

I suspect this little rule has a great deal of pertinence, even to faculty politics and curriculum matters. It has to do with student life and shared learning, with academic competition and receiving the "best call," and much else.

There is a rightful place in neighboring for asserting self and for looking after self. The utterance of complaint and the assertion of the self is as legitimate with neighbor as it is with God. It is true that "all things are lawful," and that comprehensive freedom must be asserted, insisted upon, and cherished. The dialectic of "othering," however, includes self-abandonment for the neighbor, not needing to be first or best or most advanced or having one's own way, or whatever. And so Paul speaks of "a more excellent way" that he intends for the concrete life of the church. It is a tricky thing to know when in the presence of God to sound self-asserting complaint and when to offer self-yielding praise. Covenanting is to know when to do what. In parallel fashion, with the neighbor it is right to assert one's freedom, and it is right to yield one's freedom for the neighbor. The demanding work of covenanting is to know when to do what, and that requires a thoughtful, disciplined practice of negotiation.

3. Paul (or another person by the same name) writes:

> But speaking the truth in love, we must grow up in every way into him who is the head, into Christ, from whom the whole body, joined and knit together by every ligament with which it is equipped, as each part is working properly, promotes the body's growth in building itself up in love. (Eph. 4:15-16)

This great lyrical statement commends maturity in the church that has "one Lord, one faith, one baptism, one God and Father of all" (4:5-6).

Covenanting requires maturity to be "knit together in love." As Winnicott saw so well, a very small baby cannot "other" with mother, not until there is the emergence of some elemental maturity. And with God, it takes some maturity to move readily and appropriately between complaint and praise. And so with neighbor, this visionary mandate from Ephesians requires that there be growth as the parts of the body are increasingly joined together in trust and loyalty and forgiveness. The writer understands, moreover, that such growth is not happenstance or accidental or automatic, but must be pursued with intentionality.

What such growth in maturity requires is speaking *the truth in love*. We have a difficult time holding truth and love together. My impression is that seminaries have mostly opted in recent time for love at the expense of truth, love cast in a therapeutic mode, which often is not honest love, but it is a lie that makes us all feel better. Thus, for example, it is almost impossible now to speak the truth about a student sermon, because someone might be offended, even if the practice of such dishonest love is a disservice.

Or conversely, speaking the truth constitutes nothing of growth if it is not in love. A seminary is a place always ripe for gossip and innuendo that may on occasion have some truth in it, but nothing of love. I imagine if our utterances were disciplined by "truth in love," it may be that much less would be said, and when said, spoken with more intentionality and gravity, spoken for the upbuilding of the body.

Truth in love does not mean simply using another tone of voice. Truth, when uttered in *agape,* is a changed subject, for the truth about the neighbor, as the truth about me, is an evangelical truth of both command and promise. It is a mode of truth that summons us to become whom this Thou has always summoned us to be. The growth required for such maturity is not some fuzzy, pious business, but concerns the dailiness of how we have ordered our shared life and our common identity. Imagine what it would be like if the speech of the community were knowingly speech among the baptized, speech by the baptized to the baptized. In such a context, a different mode of discourse becomes possible and legitimate, discourse that the world would not ever expect.

So I suggest that covenanting as neighbors includes:

1. solidarity at the *daily extremes of joy and sorrow,* which requires something like praise and complaint, with and for and on behalf of the neighbor;

2. *building up,* which means recasting what is permitted, the delicate dialectic of freedom and yielding for the sake of the whole; and

3. *truthful love and loving truthfulness,* which reimages us as creatures of the gospel.

V

My fifth and final point concerns a third zone of covenanting, namely the othering of self. Now it may sound odd to speak of self as other, because we tend to view self as a unified integrity with a single identity. I shall insist, however, that the self is a conundrum of fears, hurts, and hopes that most often are in important ways unsettled, conflicted, and under adjudication. And if we do not recognize that they are unsettled, conflicted, and under negotiation, it is likely because we do not know ourselves well enough. Thus Elizabeth O'Connor stands in a long tradition of Christian spirituality in speaking of "Our Many Selves."[13] And Roy Schafer more recently has shown the way in which self-disclosing and self-discerning therapy is a conversation among "the many selves of the self."[14] I shall argue that with all of this unresolve and adjudication, we get through the day because we have arrived at some covenantal arrangements, within the self or among the selves, that are often tenuous and provisional, but enough to get through the day.

This assumption of the covenanting of the self with the self is evident at least in some texts in which the self converses with the self. Thus in the familiar opening of Psalm 103, the speaker says, "Bless the Lord, O my *nephesh.*" Thus the self issues an imperative invitation to the self. And in the parable of Luke 12:16-20, Jesus has the rich man address himself by saying, "I will say to my soul (*psyche*), 'Soul, you have ample goods laid up for many years; relax, eat, drink, be merry'" (v. 19). And perhaps most

directly pertinent for our purposes, Job's classic statement of moral innocence in Job 31 begins,

> I have made a covenant (*berîth*) with my eyes. (Job 31:1)

The self covenants with a part of the self. Job's eyes promise to Job that they
will not stray to look upon a virgin.[15]

There is an interesting example of this phenomenon in Psalm 62. Verses
1 and 5 are almost parallel. Verse 1 has it this way:

> Toward Yahweh alone is my soul at peace;
>   from him help comes to me.

But in verse 5, with a slight variation, the speaker says,

> Toward Yahweh alone be at peace, my soul,
>   for from him hope comes to me.

Hans-Joachim Kraus refers to this second form as "self-encouragement,"
whereby the self addresses the self.[16]

Now I do not want to press the matter too far, because it could be
claimed that such interior conversation is only a literary device. That, however, is enough for our purposes. It is a literary device because we have no
other way in which to make available and accessible the odd conversation
that constitutes the self. I suggest that the strong, dominant self—that is, the
one that controls this conversation—is vigilant in relation to less or dimin-
ished or even censored selves that disappear from sight but never quite go
away. Moreover, these lesser selves (or if one prefers, elements of the self)
often are not assimilated or integrated into the dominant self, and so pose
an unending threat to the established "consensus self." It may be, in Job's
language, that these several selves have entered into a covenant about who
gets what, and so we manage to maintain some uneasy equilibrium in the
presentation of self to self and to neighbor and to God. Or it may be that
the settlement that operates is not one that has been negotiated, but that it
may be essentially a power play whereby the strong self has simply imposed
itself and established patterns of control and subordination with the consent of the other selves. It is nonetheless a truism among us that the self (or
a part of the self) that is repressed and feared often makes a comeback. It
happens when we "lose control," when we regress, when we commit a
"Freudian slip." And these dangerous, revealing occasions tend to occur
when the same element we so fear about self becomes evident in someone
else in a way that reminds us, evokes us, provokes us, or threatens us. The
presence of the other may evoke a mad and disconcerting scramble among
our competing selves who work for a new configuration of power, authority, and identity.

I choose a text that is not directly related to this subject, but you will see
why I think it is appropriate to our subject. In the promissory section of

Jeremiah, *The Book of Comfort,* the prophet has God say to the Judean exiles:

> He who scattered Israel will gather him,
> and he will keep him as a shepherd a flock. (Jer. 31:10)

The word pair "scatter/gather" refers, of course, to exile and to the promise of homecoming. I wish, however, to transpose the terms for our discussion of the othering of self. I take my lead from Paul Ricoeur, who has written about the scattering and gathering of images.[17] Ricoeur's insight is closely paralleled to my point, for I am speaking of the self we are able to construe imaginatively.

I propose that the baby who has an experience of omnipotence with mother is already at work on the unavoidable task of gathering self, or having self gathered. (I am not sure if the verb should be active or passive, whether we do it or find it happening to us.) Either way, the baby is the subject of the formation of a centered, sustained identity and sense of self. Such a process is slow, hard work and is essential to becoming a functioning adult. The work of gathering is a process as well of muting, silencing, disregarding, repressing, or denying some elements of the self that cannot be accommodated in the emerging centered self. This gathering is parallel to the process of self-assertion in complaint whereby one insists upon one's own rights and gathers one's self even to assertion before God.

Such gathering of self is a powerful, critical piece of work. Those who stay alive to themselves, however, may expect the realities, pressures, and vagaries of lived experience to have that gathered self assaulted, threatened, and scattered. Sometimes the scattering may be mild and fairly routine, but at other times it may be deeply severe and destabilizing. Scattering happens whenever there is a sense of displacement and disorientation, and much of the pastoral task is to be present in such situations of scattering. In that process, peripheral selves may indeed assert themselves and insist upon being heard. Some of that assertion of the peripheral self may permit frightening, threatening, ominous selves back into the conversation. But the resounding of such selves is not always a bad or negative thing, for there may also be times when the artistic or innocent self reenters the conversation after too many victories of the angry, isolated, or cynical self.

It is by no means guaranteed, but it is always hoped that this scattering of self will end in a newly gathered self. Of course we resist the scattering, because characteristically we do not imagine that there will be a new gathered self, or if there is, the heretofore dominant self senses an irreversible loss of control. But when that regathering occurs, that is, a newly gathered self emerges, the self may experience something of a homecoming, of having at last "come down where you ought to be." When that happens, however, the newly gathered self is not ever again the same as the previously gathered self, because elements of otherness, that is, other selves, have impinged and been incorporated, and perhaps have become in some ways newly decisive.

This process of scattering and gathering is threatening, hope-filled, and ongoing. We never finish with it. The process invites us to view the otherness of self as a friend to be welcomed, and not a threat to be resisted or denied. Thus the "othering" process admits of no settled self, because the self is always reengaging self in an ongoing covenanting exercise.

I cite two tests which I believe are related to this process. Again from Ephesians:

> You were taught to put away your former way of life, your old self, corrupt and deluded by its lusts, and to be renewed in the spirit of your minds, and to clothe yourselves with the new self, created according to the likeness of God, in true righteousness and holiness. (Eph. 4:22-24)
>
> . . . seeing that you have stripped off the old self with its practices, and have clothed yourselves with the new self, which is being renewed in knowledge according to the image of its creator. (Col. 3:9-10)

These two texts speak of the process of de-selfing and re-selfing human persons. The verbs are in the imperative, suggesting that the human subject has direct intentional work to do. The texts may indeed be baptismal texts, and no doubt baptism is for the Christian community the dramatic marking of the scattering and gathering of self.[18] This process is, however, in the Christian life no once-for-all matter, for otherness keeps showing itself in new ways, waiting to be incorporated and legitimated in the community of selves.

A self regathered in the gospel is an "othered self." The epistle reads this way about the self othered in the gospel:

> . . . clothe yourselves with compassion, kindness, humility, meekness, and patience. Bear with one another and, if anyone has a complaint against another, forgive each other; just as the Lord has forgiven you, so you also must forgive. Above all, clothe yourselves with love, which binds everything together in perfect harmony. And let the peace of Christ rule in your hearts, to which indeed you were called in the one body. And be thankful. (Col. 3:12-15)

A self that has learned to complain to and praise God the other, who has learned to rejoice and grieve with the otherness of the neighbor will, I imagine, be able to scatter and gather with the otherness of self. In the process, the self arrives at new settlements, new covenantal arrangements, even if they also are provisional. This process I take to be crucial for Christian faith and Christian life, and I have come to think is a primary agenda in theological education.

VI

I have wanted to insist that covenanting is a thoroughly Jewish mode of life, involved in a profound dialectic that is endlessly under way, that touches every zone of our life, and that faces into the unresolved "both/and" of our life, while refusing simplistic "either/ors."

Clearly I have not touched on formal questions of theological education, and I have not addressed power issues that are necessarily present in every community. I believe, however, that educational and administrative dimensions of life are among those in which this process of othering must happen, so that it is not confined to liturgical and pastoral activity. This covenanting process concerns every aspect of community life, because as I understand it, such a mode of life is a concrete way in which the gospel, the news of newness, is enacted.

The reality of otherness—God, neighbor, self—will not go away, but is the very source of our life. To shun that otherness by disregard or to submit to it too easily is to forego the troublesomeness of covenant that is the glory of our humanness. What is required is the readiness to be available for the other who is perceived most often as threat, but who in fact is the gift of new life for us.

I have suggested that in every zone of our life, covenanting is a process intensely dialectical:

1. With God, covenanting requires complaint and hymn, *assertion of self* and *abandonment of self.*
2. With neighbor, covenanting requires *joy and sorrow, truth in love, upbuilding* in the midst of freedom.
3. With the self, covenanting requires the readiness to receive *scattering* and the freedom for *gathering* a self that is unlike the old one, a process we often term conversion or transformation.

Such a process in every zone of our existence requires both courage and grace. It requires the courage to be fully present in insistent, asserting ways, the kind of courage that sweet Christian piety often avoids. It requires grace to yield to the other who seems to be threat but finally is friend, a grace not easy to evince in a culture of autonomous, covenanting adults. Such a practice of courage and grace permits life in all its dimensions to be made new, according to the mystery of holy threat, holy gift, and holy call.

It occurred to me that our lives, when construed in the gospel, are not unlike the bread upon which our Lord exercises his dominical verbs: He takes, he blesses, he breaks, he gives. It is the same bread when he is finished, but it has become something it was not. And so may it be with us.

In any community of faith, there are strongly held views, and party positions, and all of that. We move into the gospel in different ways at different paces, as we are able. But what a difference it makes in an evangelical community of covenanting to have it clearly understood by all members that each of us and all of us are engaged in this arduous calling of dying and being raised to new life. That common acknowledgement is urgent for doing the real and faithful work of theological education. But beyond that, such a common understanding and common practice may be a sign in the world. You see, the world does not know about or trust the process of othering. The world does not know that there is gain in loss, that humbling invites exaltation, that the last become first, that the hungry are filled with good things and the rich sent empty away. And so we grow more fearful, more greedy, and more brutal. That greediness, fearfulness, and brutality, so evident in our society, infests the church, albeit around slightly different issues. The world does not believe that the courage and grace of othering make any difference on our passionate road to death. But we know "a more excellent way."

I conclude these comments with two poignant statements from 1 John which attend to this glorious process of lived faith in which the zones of life I have identified are intensely linked to each other:

> We know that we have passed from death to life because we love one another. Whoever does not love abides in death. (3:14)
> Those who do not love a brother or sister whom they have seen, cannot love God whom they have not seen. (4:20)

2

The Daily Voice of Faith:
The Covenanted Self

COMING TO TERMS WITH THIS SURPRISING THOU REQUIRES IN OUR LIFE the full-ranged dialectic of lament and hymn, a dialectic anticipatory of the relation of crucifixion and resurrection, which Moltmann terms "the dialectic of reconciliation."[1] I have argued that lament concerns the *full assertion of self over against God* and praise concerns the *full abandonment of self to God*. This drama of assertion and abandonment is indispensable for life with this God.[2]

The full drama is nonetheless inordinately demanding. It is demanding because in this two-fold drama, we (and this surprising Thou) are always changing positions and reversing roles. In a voice of lament, we may occupy a position of authority over against God and dare to address God in insistent imperative. This is an awkward posture for us and, even if necessary, we sense its peculiar inappropriateness. By contrast, in a voice of praise we occupy a posture of glad subordination to God, and address God in God's full authority. Moving back and forth between lament and praise means always shifting positions, getting up out of our seat and changing roles, sometimes moving quickly in a single poem or song, in a single voice or utterance. Live communion with an initiating and responsive Thou requires precisely such vitality, energy, freedom, and courage.

Each of us, I imagine, would prefer one of these roles to the other. Conventionally, many of us who have learned to submit to authority would rather sing hymns of praise and adoration, would rather keep doing this even in the face of cognitive dissonance, even if we have to engage in profound denial in order to keep the positive song going, even if we sing through clinched teeth, or finally find the cover-up too burdensome. When it is too burdensome and we cannot bear any longer to praise, we may hire soloists and pay people to do it for us, because we can no longer force the songs out of our stricken mouths. Hymns by themselves may often encourage denial and yield the sounds of a false self uttering words and sounds not rooted in a genuine self.

Many of us, conversely, who have become cynical with and restless against authority, may find such praise intolerable. We may prefer to channel our God-talk into endless self-preoccupation, continuing endless lament and complaint. In such a habit, we continually sit in the driver's seat for the relationship, keeping the initiative for ourselves, speaking only in shrill, insistent imperative. That way, taken alone, results in self-indulgence and narcissism, imagining that my grievances are the very center of reality.

Thus without this dialectic of complaint and praise, that is, a "dialectic of reconciliation," we end either in *denial* of self and reality for the sake of God, or in *self-indulgence*, which trivializes God into our therapist or whipping boy. Either of these alternatives, taken alone, precludes the kind of liveliness and honesty that properly belongs to this relation, and perverts the kind of communion proposed in biblical faith between two centers of power and will, centers made for each other but in starkly incommensurate ways.

1

In what follows, we consider the outcome of a *life of communion*, that is, of intentional, dialectical interaction, in which there is the full practice of both assertion and abandonment. To what end is all this song-singing addressed to this Thou who is definitional for our existence? In the first instance, this dialectic of assertion and abandonment is the thing itself. That is what life consists in, and we need not ask further about its intention or purpose. Indeed, if we have to ask about its meaning we clearly do not understand and will never understand, because the process itself is the purpose. Engagement with God in this dialectic is the very enactment of evangelical existence.

We arrive then at an awareness that a Jewish understanding of self vis-à-vis God, a quite peculiar understanding, is one of intense *interactionism*, marked by a sort of mutuality, even if not commensurability. First, a historical observation. Hans Urs von Balthasar has observed: "In 1919, one of the strangest phenomenon of 'acausal contemporaneity' in the history of the intellect took place."[3] This was the simultaneous emergence of the "dialogical principle in the thinkers who could not be further apart." That is, in the same year five scholars, seemingly independent from each other, came up with the same fresh assertion about the nature of reality. The best known of these is Martin Buber, *I and Thou*, in which an "I" emerges only because of a "Thou."[4] The list of scholarly contributors to this remarkable convergence include Buber's associate Franz Rosenzweig, Rosenzweig's conversation partner Eugen Rosenstock-Huessey, as well as the great Catholic Gabriel Marcel, and a German who wrote only one book, Ferdinand Ebner.[5] "The dialogical principle" is the insistence that the self is always a self in relation and therefore reality is at core a relational interaction, that is, no autonomous, fixed, self-sufficient self. Most radically the principle may even suggest that not even God may be understood as an autonomous, self-sufficient agent, but is always known in a relational interaction that impinges even upon the character of God. Subsequently Emmanuel Levinas has built his philosophical program around the principle of "otherness," that is, Buber's "Thou."[6] Reference should also be made to George Steiner who makes "alterity" the principle of his argument concerning the relation between God and great literature.[7] That is, for Steiner, God is the other who permits and evokes great literature. It is difficult to imagine a more radical, more breathtaking model of reality, a model that fights against every sense of an autonomous, sealed-off self, or in scholastic theology, even a sealed-off God. It is my impression that this principle of interactionism, which is crucial for biblical understandings of reality, has been largely disregarded in conventional theology and is enormously important for a theology and practice of faithful ministry.

Along with this philosophical approach to the dialogical principle from the 1920s, interactionism has received a second different, but quite important, articulation in personality theory, which at the outset had no interest at all in theology.[8]

II

Now on the basis of that *philosophical articulation* of Buber and his contemporaries and the *psychological discernment* of Object Relations theorists, I want to consider the outcome in biblical faith of a self that is fully asserted and fully abandoned. A life lived in a dialectic of *assertion* and *abandonment* is one in which *obedience* is a practice of *freedom* that culminates in *communion*. Notice that I have put *obedience, freedom,* and *communion* in the same sentence. I suggest that this lively, dialectic communion is the ground that makes possible the joyous juxtaposition of obedience and freedom.

Finally, because God is incommensurately God, the matter of communion with God in Israel must come to obedience. As this communion partakes of something like *mutuality*, in the very midst of mutuality Israel recognizes that the parties to communion are *not commensurate*. The God addressed in complaint and praise is *God*, and so will command as well as empathize.[9] Most largely understood, our discernment of self issues in obedience, because this Jewish community knows itself to be under command, and knows that the one addressed in lament and hymn is the one who issues commands.[10]

More specifically, while the Psalter is largely constituted by laments and hymns, the corpus of the Psalter, as James L. Mays has seen, is framed, arranged, and ordered in its "final form" by reflection upon the Torah, especially in the beginning with Psalm 1, and in Psalm 119 which many scholars (following Claus Westermann) have seen to be a conclusion for a certain point in the canonizing process.[11] Mays, Gerald H. Wilson, and a number of scholars have seen that the completed Psalter is instruction in "Torah piety," that is, a devotional practice (we would say "spirituality") that is preoccupied with Yahweh's commands.[12] My beginning point here is that laments of assertion and hymns of abandonment are the required and indispensable practices whereby this community of covenant makes itself ready and keeps itself ready for obedience to the commands of the "other," the "Thou" who gives life.

In approaching this theme of obedience, we do well to consider the ways in which obedience has become a problematic notion in our contemporary practice of faith and piety. The story whereby obedience has become problematic is a very old one. We may cite two unmistakable examples of the problem of obedience in Israel's Scripture, examples that may function as models for two practices that fail to arise from a necessary and healthy dialectic. First, Job's friends are a recognizable caricature of the obedient abandonment of self. They are advocates for every kind of obedience and believe that obedience should be in every case unquestioning. They are willing to give themselves over to God at great cost to themselves, indeed at full cost to themselves, in order that (among other things) God's honor and justice should be protected and remain unquestioned. It is inconceivable that Job's friends should ever utter a lament that would assert a right over against God. They are in this way quite unlike Job, who complained freely,[13] who refused to reduce his life to the problem of guilt. Vigorous lament is able to entertain the notion that the breakdown of moral equity may be in the failure of God. Such a possibility the friends will not entertain, and so their obedience—without lament—is graceless. We may imagine that such graceless obedience is inappropriate to this God.

Second, at the other end of the dialectic, we may cite Psalm 106 as an example of a refusal to praise. In this psalm, Israel's entire history is construed as an account of amnesia, ingratitude, and rebellion. Israel is incapable of noticing or crediting God's miracles, and so of course, being grimly self-preoccupied, had nothing for which to render to God thanks and praise. Or a personal parallel is the "fool" in Psalms 9 and 10 who is unable or unwilling to acknowledge God. He says in his heart, "There is no God" (Ps. 10:4) and then undertakes a life of oppressive exploitation (Ps. 10:8-10). The alternative to self-yielding praise is a self-sufficiency that becomes a law until itself.

These examples show in turn a *graceless obedience* (Job's friends) incapable of self-asserting lament but ready to reduce life to formulary submissiveness, and *praiseless autonomy* (Pss. 9, 10, 106), which knows nothing of gratitude and which ends inevitably in exploitation. It may be argued that of these alternatives, the former is preferable, for at least it is obedience. Job's friends did better than the fool in Psalm 10 or Israel in Psalm 106. More likely, however, such obedience is deathly and destructive and is no real gain. In any case, moreover, both such practices miss the wonder, mystery, and miracle that belong to a life of genuine covenantal interaction. Both yield a life in which joyous Torah piety is an impossibility. I imagine that each of us in personal and peculiar ways is tempted either to *graceless obedience* or to *praiseless autonomy*, or to both.

III

The problematic character of obedience as we experience it, however, may not be as old as we imagine it to be. It is at least clear that the ancient world of Jews who put the Hebrew Bible/Old Testament into its present form was not excessively troubled by obedience.[14] Because the Psalter as Israel's hymn book is framed for Torah piety, there is no hint that Genesis 3 was regarded as a decisive "fall" into disobedience, as it has become in normative (Pauline) Christian theology.[15]

It may well be that Luther's profound negative toward "the law" has been decisive in making obedience a negative in the modern world, and surely has been a caricature of Judaism.[16] Whatever we may make of Luther's contribution, the works of Descartes and Locke are surely decisive in forming modern consciousness against any notion of obedience to the law.[17] The modern ideal has been a "turn to the subject," which celebrated unmitigated freedom requiring the rejection of every authoritative tradition, including all traditions containing any notion of command and obedience. Such a notion of the autonomous agent, featured in Kant's "Man Come of Age," was not answerable to any commandment given. No doubt it is a leap from Luther to the Enlightenment, but there is continuity in seeing the emancipation of the individual from the power of "law." As this formulation of the notion of autonomous agent became normative, Freud entered the lists for freedom from command, with the proposal that maturity entails escape from, or destruction of, authority figures.

Of course Descartes, Locke, Kant, or Freud cannot be held accountable for all that came after them. We can nonetheless see the connections whereby autonomy came to be regarded as good and submission to authority as bad.[18] This modern tendency finally has issued in what is now termed "the therapeutic culture," (not to be confused with the practice of serious therapy), in which the subject is endlessly fascinated with self without any reference points outside the self.[19] The outcome of this programmatic development of course has been a self-indulgent society in which the disciplines of neighborliness, that is, attention to the other, have disappeared. In place of neighborhood has come mall. Indeed, Adam Smith understood that expanding markets depend upon the generation of desire, which culminates in consumerism that has no point of contact with the serious engagement of "other" that so marks covenantal interaction.[20]

Our particular practice of such anti-neighborliness in the church is a situation in which moral authority has devolved into negotiations between interest groups, each of which holds its own interest to be the ultimate norm for deployment of church energy and finally the criterion for what is true. The notion of emancipated autonomy has succeeded, until there has come a disappearance of the other as a point of reference. There is, then, no other to whom to address complaint, or to whom to sing praise, or finally from whom to receive command. God has vanished, either in a mindless conformity or in a limitless narcissism. And when God has vanished, the neighbor quickly disappears.

It is not, I take it, excessively alarmist to say that we cannot go on like this. But my point is not an alarmist one. It is rather to insist that biblical faith in its "processes of selfhood" understands the emergence and maintenance of self very differently from our contemporary dominant notions, precisely because biblical rhetoric and biblical sensitivity do not entertain the banishment of this commanding Thou who will not be banished (cf. Amos 9:2-4, Ps. 139:7-12). The reason for the recovery of commandment is not simply our current social crisis, but rather the recognition of the true character of human existence in the face of this Other who does indeed command. A true self is a self under command. Thus I suggest that attention to biblical processes of the self is crucial if we are to find a way alternative to the increasingly dysfunctional and destructive modes of autonomy (without self-abandonment) and conformity (without self-assertion) that are so powerful all around us.

IV

This is, then, a reflection upon Yahweh's commands in Israel, and Israel's *receptivity* to them and *resistance* to them. I make no further reference to the crisis of modernity and postmodernity, but I hope and assume that the parallels and analogues I intend will be as clear to you as they are to me.

The story of commandment in Israel is based on the normative memory of Exodus and Sinai. Israel's shaping memory, for all time to come, is the memory of the time in servitude in Egypt. This family of covenant went to Egypt because there was a famine in the land of promise (odd enough!). They went to the place (the only place?) that had bread (Gen. 12:10). It is not at all odd that Egypt had bread, for the empire practiced a demanding, greedy monopoly of grain and food. The ancestors of Israel went to Egypt in order to be fed by the monopoly. They were fed, but the food cost them in turn their cattle, their land, and finally their freedom (Gen. 47:13-26). The monopoly that devoured them was devised and presided over by their kinsman Joseph, who did not flinch from the cost of servitude for his own family (Gen. 47:10-12, 27-28). He exacted from them the price always exacted by the monopoly.

Israel went for bread. Along with bread Israel soon got a harsh, single, all-encompassing commandment: "Make bricks!" "Make more bricks!" "Make them and gather your own straw for them" (Exod. 1:11-14, 5:16-19). From the outset, this people Israel has been under command, even though it never voted itself into that status or gave consent for servitude. The command is not given by Yahweh. It is given by this other, more demanding task-master, Pharaoh, the one who knew not Joseph, who did not care for Israel at all, but cared only for his precious, self-aggrandizing building program.

Into such a context came the burning bush, Moses, and the possibility of rescue from slavery (Exod. 3:1-6). The break in the imperial command of bricks came from a God whose name they had not known (Exod. 3:13-15). Pharaoh did not know this challenging God (Exod. 5:2), nor did Israel, nor did even Moses. Yahweh (the best version of the name now given for God) did not lie to this bondaged people. Yahweh never promised or even suggested autonomy as the outcome of the Exodus. From the beginning, Yahweh intended that Israel should be in "bondage" to the commands of Yahweh. From the first utterance, Yahweh had consistently said, "Let them go, that they may *serve* me" (5:1). Consistently the governing verb is "serve" (*abad*), "enter into my service." (Occasionally the alternative verb *hag* is used, "make a festival.") Yahweh never said, "Let my people go that they may be autonomous," or "Let my people go that they may enjoy unmitigated freedom." "That they may serve me" means to come under a sovereign command. Thus the "freed slaves" have a freedom that is a new servitude, under new commands and new demands.

By the hard way of the wilderness (Exod. 16-18), Israel arrived at Sinai (19:1). Israel had as yet no particular details of what the new regime would require. But Israel knew the new regime had to be better than Pharaoh's brick quotas. As you know, the commands of Yahweh, as alternative to the demands of Pharaoh, are not given until Exod. 20:1-17. A very strange thing, however, happens in Exodus 19, prior to the promulgation of the commands. In that preparatory chapter, God says to Moses:

> Now therefore, if you obey my voice and keep my covenant, you shall be my treasured possession out of all the peoples. Indeed, the whole earth is mine, but you shall be for me a priestly kingdom and a holy nation. These are the words that you shall speak to the Israelites. (vv. 5-6)

That is all: "Obey my voice" (with an infinitive absolute), "Keep my covenant" (with an infinitive absolute); there are no details, no particulars, no specific commands.

Oddly enough, when this statement is reported by Moses to Israel (19:7), the people respond:

> Everything that the Lord has spoken we will do. (v. 8)

Israel agreed to the requirement of their new commander and sovereign! They signed on willingly for this alternative. They signed a blank check. They agreed to the commands of Yahweh, even without knowing what they were. They did so, perhaps, because anything would be better than Pharaoh, or because they had come to trust this God of liberation. In any case, that blind act of allegiance has been decisive for this community ever since. From this odd act onward, Jews have been "children of command," as have their belated kin, Christians and Muslims. This theological relation is defined by command, and there is no doubt about the structure of sovereignty and subordination, a relation willingly accepted and agreed to by Israel.

After this initial vow of fidelity in 19:8, after careful preparation and negotiation (19:10-25), Yahweh speaks to Israel directly—ten times! (20:1-17). Ten times and not more. That is all. And that for Israel is everything.

Ten list Commandment

You know these commands that used to be the central staple of the catechism, before Enlightenment emancipation eroded the nerve of the church, back when the church was willing to speak to its children about obedience. You know the commands: three on the holiness of God; six on the requirements of viable social life concerning parents, neighbors, courts, and property; and one in the middle on "rest" as the goal and purpose of life.

That is all. And the way the Bible is set up, Yahweh never gives any more commands directly. The rest is the exposition of Moses, for immediately in Exod. 20:18-21, Israel comes in its anxiety to Moses and says, "Let's don't ever do that again. It's too scary. From now on, it's you Moses to whom we will listen." And so they agreed.

As it turned out, these ten words were enough. It is the intent of this set of ten words to bring every zone of life under the rule of Yahweh, that is, to wrest zone by zone from the aegis of Pharaoh, perhaps to claim zone by zone from the unadministered chaos of no command, for such unadministered freedom is seen to issue in idolatry, oppression, and chaos. But that is not said in the text. The contrast to the commands of Pharaoh is much more immediate in the narrative than is the contrast to unadministered autonomy.

The commands of Sinai intend that all of life should be devoted to the · Lord of the covenant. I do not defend these commands or seek to justify them. Certainly they have been subject to incredible authoritarian abuse,[21] and certainly they have required endless interpretation and renegotiation.[22] For now we may leave all of that aside, in order to note that the commands are a given for Israel, however we may interpret. The commands of Yahweh contrast sharply with the commands of Pharaoh, for at the center is a "sabbath" and not "bricks." They are, moreover, an act of grace, for now Israel knows what is required by Yahweh. Israel does not have to guess or to wait for more guidance (cf. Deut. 30:11-14). And as the text has it, this set of commands tells about the very character of God, the creator of heaven and earth, the liberator of Israel, the God disclosed in Jesus of Nazareth. These are not mere rules, but a theological datum about the covenant of the God of Israel. It is on Yahweh's mind that these commands are to set Yahweh and the Israelite operation apart from Pharaoh:

> They are my servants, whom I brought out of the land of Egypt;
> they shall not be sold as slaves are sold. (Lev. 25:42)

Of course the commands are not only a theological datum concerning the character of God. The commands are also a declaration of fundamental social policy. The antithesis between the Egyptian gods (cf. Exod. 12:12) and Yahweh, the God of the Exodus, has its inescapable counter-part in the contrasting social intentionalities of Egyptian imperial policy marked by monopoly and exploitation, and the will of Yahweh marked by covenantal egalitarianism. Norman Gottwald has seen most clearly that the commands at Sinai pertain to a radical reordering of social relations and the potential-ly life-giving role and function of social structures and social institutions.[23] Gottwald is often critiqued for having overstated the case for egalitarian-ism, and the critique may in part be correct. However, all of the potential for egalitarianism in these commands need not be explicit. One may indeed argue that through the prophetic and Deuteronomic traditions, the Torah practice of Ezra and Nehemiah, and finally the covenantal accents of Calvinism that eventuated in Puritan theories of democratic society, Sinai did unleash in the world a genuine alternative to hierarchical, stratified monopoly.[24]

The Bible of course does not make all this explicit at Sinai. Indeed, the commands of Sinai are so terse and so familiar to us that it is possible to hear them as simply flat rules that can be understood in legalistic ways, without seeing that they are a summons to, and authorization for, member-ship in a quite alternative society, a society that dares to claim itself to be en route to the "kingdom of God." Moses at Sinai thus states a deep either/or. When one embraces Yahweh, one embraces not only a very different God, but also membership in a very different social practice.

V

As many scholars now believe, it is likely that the Exodus-Sinai portrayal of the Bible is primarily an ideological construct, that is, we cannot know what if any historicity lies behind these traditions.[25] If it is an ideological construct, then we may ask what end and purpose that ideology intends to serve. The tradition of command in the Sinai portrayal of sociotheological reality is intended to fund and authorize Israel's covenantal tradition as practiced in the Deuteronomic-prophetic tradition. Dominant critical opin-ion is that "covenantal ideology" really only becomes visible and articulate in the seventh century.[26] In the time related to Deuteronomy, we may also place Hosea and Jeremiah as the principle voices of Torah theology, the same Torah theology that turns up as Torah piety in the Psalter. Thus the Torah piety of the Psalms, endlessly available to worshipping Israel, serves to keep Sinai's commands palpably contemporary.

The Torah tradition that understood life as under the counter-command of Yahweh is kept alive as a critical response to the dominant practice of Israelite life under the Jerusalem monarchy. It seems clear, and I shall not argue here, that the Davidic-Solomonic monarchy, with its accompanying temple theology, in practice if not in theory embraced in wholesale ways the oppressive, monopolistic, self-indulgence that marked the world of Pharaoh.[27] That is, the monarch, as the central agent of public power, utilized power in conventional ways, mostly not worse than elsewhere, but mostly not better than elsewhere. And like all public forms of power, the monarchy had a supportive religious ideology that made its practices sound better than they were.

My point here is not to analyze or critique royal modes of power, but to consider the challenge to these modes of power that was voiced by the Torah tradition of Deuteronomy, Hosea, Jeremiah, and the Psalter, the primal ongoing voice of command.

The most forceful articulation of this tradition is in Deuteronomy, which presents itself as having direct connections to Moses. The Book of Deuteronomy, a primary deposit of Torah piety, does not claim to have its setting at Sinai, but is many years later at the edge of the Jordan as Israel finally is about to enter the land of promise (Deut. 1:1). While the ten commands of Sinai are reiterated in Deut. 5:6-21, they do no more than mark the beginning point for the reflection of Deuteronomy. This book is a remembering of Sinai, but it is not a *pro forma* reiteration of Sinai. Rather, Deuteronomy is a vigorous and imaginative re-remembering, that is, reinterpretation of Torah for a new time, place, and circumstance. As Gerald Sheppard has seen, Deuteronomy makes clear the relentless vitality and dynamic of Mosaic Torah, so that the Torah is not closed and settled.[28] Rather "Moses" reshapes command to meet new circumstance and in noticeable ways introduces quite new subject matter into the Torah, in order to bring new zones of life under the Torah intentionality of Yahweh. This point is exceedingly important, because it is often not understood among us, as the commands are taken much too frequently as closed and flat.

In the book of Deuteronomy, Moses pauses very long at the river Jordan, at the brink of the new land. He pauses and requires Israel to wait, just at the moment when Israel is most eager to go, much too restless to wait. I imagine that the tension between eager Israel and pausing Moses is not unlike the last desperate conversation before a parent sends one's first child off to college. The parent knows the venture of college is ominous and loaded with anxiety, but the child is not listening, excessively eager for a surge of unmitigated freedom.

The new place to which this community of covenant is to go is "the land of Canaan." The term "Canaan" (or "Canaanite"), it is agreed, is not an ethnic term.[29] It is an ideological term, used by Israel to characterize all those who refuse Israel's vision of covenantal reality and who are committed to rapacious, exploitative, monopolistic social policy and practice. The insistence of Deuteronomy is simple. Israelites under Yahweh's Torah are not Canaanites, are not to become Canaanites, and may not participate in

Canaanite social policy or practice. The long speech of Moses in Deuteronomy seeks to assert and establish Israel's oddity, an oddity both theological
and sociopolitical, an oddity defined by and insisted upon by the Torah of
Moses.

But the long speech of Moses in Deuteronomy also has a positive intention. In Deuteronomy Moses is buoyant and confident about the potential
for the effectiveness of the Torah in the new land. Moses believes that the
land of Canaan does not need to remain "Canaanite," that is, governed by
exploitative, oppressive social practices. The obedience of Israel is to
reorder the public life of Canaan in covenantal, more nearly egalitarian
ways. Thus the very land which is a seductive threat is also a powerful
opportunity for reform and reordering. Moses introduces quite new teaching into the Torah, that was not on the horizon of Sinai, concerning a court
system, a monarchy, prophecy, and a host of other practices which will
make life in the new land an enactment of the will of the liberating God of
the Exodus.[30]

Everything, however, depends upon Israel's obedience to the command.
Everything depends upon Israel's willingness to listen, and to respond in
ways that exhibit the holiness of God and the reality of the neighbor. This
dynamic voicing by Moses, rooted in Exodus, authorized at Sinai, and
exposited in Deuteronomy, is the peculiar characterization of Israel as a people of Torah, authorized to live a different kind of life in the world for the
sake of the world. It is an authorization that summons Israel away from the
coerciveness of Pharaoh and away from the self-indulgence of Canaan. It is
impossible to overstate the cruciality of this Torah for the faith of Israel, and
I believe, impossible to overstate its cruciality for the future of the world.

VI

I have spent a long time on these perhaps obvious "traditions of command"
which define Israel. I have done so in order to reflect upon the capacity for
obedience to Torah in a social milieu that wants to scuttle the commands, a
social milieu like that in which we live. It is of course a long jump from the
great model of Moses in the Pentateuch to the advocacy of the Torah piety
of the Psalms. It is a move from great public models to quite intimate and
personal decisions. It is a move from great generative events in ancient
Israel to what is likely the modesty and specificity of postexilic poetry. The
question I want to ask is: What made it possible for Israel, late in this telling
of its life, in circumstances very different from those of Moses, circumstances in which it was easy to conclude (as did Qoheleth) that the great
claims of faith had failed, to continue to "meditate day and night on the
Torah" (Ps. 1:2, cf. Deut. 17:19)?

My answer is this. Serious, supple, imaginative, inventive, liberated obedience to the commands can only take place in the midst of a dialectic of

asserting and abandoning self, in an endless drama of claiming and ceding self. Or said another way, the continued *voice of Friday* (or protest and insistence) and the continued *voice of Sunday* (of glad praise and doxology) makes possible *the daily voice* of obedience that is embraced with a glad and full heart. Obedience is the daily voice of faith because on all days, days of plenty and want, of richness and poverty, in sickness and in health, faith shows up as obedience. And without this continual dialectic, obedience will become either grudging coerciveness or romantic emancipation, neither of which makes human life possible. It is my judgment that the church in our time and place, while it continues to do these psalms, has lost the substance of the dialectic, and therefore we quarrel endlessly somewhere between coerciveness and emancipation, neither of which comes close to the reality of covenant.

I cite four examples of this dialectical process whereby people of faith can process their life in open, joyous response to the command of God.

1. *Abraham, great model of faith.* The rabbis have often noticed and commented upon the odd juxtaposition between Gen. 18:22-32 and Gen. 22:1-14.[31] In Gen. 18, Abraham stubbornly and boldly stands up to Yahweh, chastens God about God's propensity to injustice, and instructs God in the ways of justice. Abraham holds his own with Yahweh, at least as an equal partner.[32] In chapter 22, however, this same Abraham is presented as a model of submissive faith, prepared to give up even his only beloved son at the command of God. We would not have expected in chapter 18 that Abraham would be prepared for such obedience. It is my urging, however, that it is precisely the courage of Abraham in chapter 18 that makes possible his radical obedience in chapter 22.

2. *Moses is the quintessential agent of obedience in Israel,* not only the giver of command, but the hard-nosed enforcer whose life is one of obedience. Most astonishingly, Moses' prayers in Exod. 32–33 and Numbers 11 are among the most daring and demanding in all of Scripture.[33] Moses dares to confront Yahweh and to urge God to specific action, and frequently to move Yahweh to actions that God had not intended to take. For example, in Num. 14:13-20 Moses in fact shames Yahweh into an action of forgiveness when God's own propensity was to destroy. The freedom and courage of Moses in God's presence, I submit, make possible his readiness to be in covenant with the God who commands and who must be obeyed.

3. *Jeremiah is portrayed as the paradigm of the covenanting prophet.*[34] It is he, as presented to us, who most insists upon obedience and who most uses the imperative term *shema.* Oddly enough, this great Torah-prophet is also the voice of the most shrill complaint and lamentation of any of the prophets.[35] Jeremiah is, as Walter Baumgartner has shown, a genuine child of the Psalter, fully at home in the psalms of complaint and prepared to make them his very own.[36] In Jer. 20:7-13, his last and most shrill complaint, Jeremiah begins in v. 7 with a harsh accusation against Yahweh who

has "seduced" him. By v. 13, in the same speech, the prophet is moved to praise:

> Sing to the Lord;
>   praise the Lord!
> For he has delivered the life of the needy
>   from the hands of evildoers.

This development from v. 7 to v. 13 follows the normal development from plea to praise, as Westermann has outlined it. But if we are to take the complaint as the real speech of a real person (and not simply a characteristic form), I suggest it is the freedom and intimacy of the complaint that makes possible the extravagance of doxology that in turn readies the prophet for obedience. To be sure, the following verses of 20:14-18 show the speaker in terrible despair, indicating that the relationship is fluid, and the move from complaint to praise is not a permanent gain. But openness of this sort is precisely what happens in such a drama of covenant.

4. Finally we come to *Job, the most extreme case of our drama of covenant.* The poem of Job, as is often noticed, is cast in noncovenantal categories in a way that shows few marks of Israel's faith. Nonetheless, attention to the genres of speech shows that the same drama of *self with other* is underway here. Job is a vociferous accuser of God, so that even his name "Job" means "adversary," that is, adversary to God. Westermann has shown that much of Job's speech is in the form of complaint against the dysfunction of Yahweh's part in the covenant.[37] But then there is this overpowering doxology in the mouth of Yahweh (Job 38-41), which culminates in Job's full, even if enigmatic, surrender to Yahweh in 42:6:

> Therefore I despise myself
>   and repent in dust and ashes.

Thus the sequence of complaint, doxology, and submission occurs yet again.[38] And in 42:7-8, this protesting man is said by the doxology-singing God to have spoken what is "right." The completed presentation of Job exhibits the sequence of complaint and praise as a drama appropriate to this one who remains in the eyes of God (and the book of Job) "blameless and upright" (Job 1:1, 8, 2:3), as "blameless and upright" at the end of the drama as at the beginning. We may take that descriptive endorsement of "blameless and upright," in Israel's large reading, as meaning commitment to Torah. It is the very drama modeled by Job that permits Torah obedience that is neither grudging nor rebellious.

In all four cases I have cited, these models of obedience practice the full dialectic of assertion and abandoning, of claiming and ceding, of Friday and Sunday, which makes life under command not only possible, but full, energized, joyous, and unreserved.

VII

In the end, my intent here is quite practical and pastoral. I am concerned with this issue: In a society bouncing between coercive conformity, Christopher Bollas's "normotic personality,"[39] and self-sufficient self authorization, how are persons of faith to practice Torah piety? How is there to be a community under command to covenant, a community upon which the health of the world and the joy of heaven depend?

It is my impression that in its pastoral, liturgical life, the church has forgotten this dialectic of personhood that is pervasive in the biblical tradition. And having failed to value and make available this two-fold, endlessly reenacted practice of claiming and ceding, the church has given up on the task of covenanting and has settled instead, according to our several ideological interests, for either *coercive conformity* or *detached autonomy*. In so doing, moreover, we have given up most of our gift and much of our task.

The real issues of covenanting are likely not to emerge in specific commands, or behaviors, or policies; the real issues are the *imaginative processes of protest and praise,* which make a person fit for glad obedience. As we have learned in responsible therapeutic practice and occasionally in liturgy, the full freedom to live these relational extremities makes possible a resolve for a new righteousness that is not imposed or extrinsic, and therefore not coercive. The new righteousness arises out of the health and liveliness of a full interaction that spills from Friday over into Sunday and then into every day.

Thus the psalmists advocate Torah piety, which "meditates on the Torah day and night." The voice of such Torah piety is able to assert with a full heart, "Oh, how I love your Torah" (Ps. 119:97) who experiences Torah as "wonderful" (Ps. 119:129) and "just" (v. 149), and finally as an arena of "liberty" (v. 45). To arrive at such an affirmative posture is not easy or quick or obvious. It comes only as a consequence of a life of daring protest and exuberant praise, until abrasiveness becomes intimacy, until adversarial postures turn into friendship, until the one who seems to impose is known to be the giver of the best, healthiest freedom available.

In the end, the obedience of Torah piety is not "must" or "ought" or "should." It is rather the kind of delight whereby friendship ripens into love, and obligation is the chance to please and delight the other, the Thou who hopes and delights in us, as well as commands us. It is this strange process, whereby duty becomes delight without ceasing to be duty, that is expressed in *Simhat Torah*, the festival of the "joy of the Torah."

I finish with two texts and then two contemporary *midrashim* upon obedience as an act of willing, joyous devotion.

1. *Jeremiah 31:31-43.* This well-known text is an anticipation of the reconstituted community of covenant after the exile. Only by bold extrapolation does the new covenant concern Jesus and the church.[40] Properly it concerns

the readiness of God to re-love the community of Sinai. The text character-
izes the newly shaped covenant in several ways:

- "I will be their God, and they shall be my people" (v. 33). This is a
  statement of intimacy, solidarity, and mutually exclusive loyalty, that
  is, a relation of trust that will work as the old pattern of Sinai did not.
- "They shall all know me from the last to the greatest" (v. 34). They
  shall all acknowledge Yahweh, trust, serve, and know the purpose of
  Yahweh. No one will resist and none shall lord it over any other.
- "I will forgive them their iniquity, and remember their sin no more"
  (v. 34). The exilic community is burdened with guilt. Now that entire
  past is to be nullified and overcome by the compassion and passion of
  Yahweh in this act of beginning again.

Important as these points are, I refer to this text because of a fourth motif:

> I will put my Torah in their midst
> and I will write it upon their hearts (v. 33).

As you know, heretofore the Torah had been written on tablets, external to
the members of the community. The phrasing of "write on their hearts," as
in Prov. 6:20-22, likely is first of all to be taken literally:

> My child, keep your father's commandment,
>   and do not forsake your mother's teaching.
> Bind them upon your heart always;
>   tie them around your neck.
> When you walk, they will lead you;
>   when you lie down, they will watch over you;
>   and when you awake, they will talk with you.

The image refers to a copy of the commandments tied around the neck,
much as one may wear a cross or a good luck piece, a charm or an identifi-
cation marker. This copy was presumably kept very close and worn all the
time, so that it goes wherever the person goes, and the person is never without it. The copy of the Torah that dangles over the heart is inseparable from
the person.

Then, however, as in our text, the phrasing no doubt has become a
metaphor. It means that the commands are to be ingested into one's identity, internalized, taken as one's own and part of one's self, of one's heart.
Obedience then is not to an external other as though imposed. Rather obedience comes to be one's heart's desire, a way to please the beloved becomes
an inclination of the heart. The Enlightenment notion of command as
imposition is completely absent here. In this new relation of covenant, the
command is heart's desire, manifestation of true self, and one cannot want
to do otherwise, because disobedience becomes a violation of one's own
self. This is indeed Torah piety wherein the Torah of Yahweh is an arena of
liberty, in which re-loved Israel rejoices.

2. In *Mark 10:17-22* the person with many possessions asked Jesus about the obedience that leads to life. Characteristically Jewish, Jesus' first answer concerns obedience to the Torah commands, an obedience this man has fully embraced. Jesus' second answer, however, is an invitation to make obedience one's true heart's desire that will let one abandon all for the sake of companionship:

> You lack one thing; go, sell what you own, and give the money to the poor, and you will have treasure in heaven; then come, follow me. (v. 21)

This summons, of course, the man rejects, for he is not so smitten by companionship with Jesus as to abandon all else. Some of us struggle to do the first set of commands, but they are external and extrinsic. Some of us do that set of commands approximately, but either in conformity or in autonomy; "command-cum-communion" is not yet our true heart's desire. We have not yet moved through the drama of trusting friendship that makes everything else irrelevant. But such willing devotion is possible; it is possible, says Jesus, because "for God all things are possible" (v. 27).

3. Archbishop William Temple, in one of his stunning aphorisms, has said that true joy happens when *what one must do* converges with *what one most wants to do*. I submit that Torah piety celebrates that convergence in which commandment is not simply a "must," but is a glad, chosen "want," for one craves nothing more than communion in mutuality, which depends upon obedience to this incommensurate one.

4. Frederick Buechner, in his remarkable statement on vocation, has written:

> There are all kinds of voices calling you to all different kinds of work, and the problem is to find out which is the voice of God rather than of society, say, or the Superego, or Self Interest.
>
> By and large a good rule for finding out is this. The kind of work God usually calls you to is the kind of work (a) that you need to do and (b) that the world most needs to have done. If you really get a kick out of your work, you've presumably met requirement (a), but if your work is writing TV deodorant commercials, the chances are you've missed requirement (b). On the other hand, if your work is being a doctor in a leper colony, you have probably met requirement (b), but if most of the time you're bored and depressed by it, the chances are you have not only bypassed (a) but probably aren't healing your patients either.
>
> Neither the hair shirt nor the soft berth will do. The place God calls you is the place where your deep gladness and the world's deep hunger meet.[41]

Just so! That convergence is the quintessence of mature spirituality. But as long as there is a gap between "must" and "want," between need and desire, command will be imposed, and alienation becomes inevitable.

Karl Marx understood the deep alienation that marks modern life. It is not only alienation between self and work, as Marx saw so well, but it is the larger alienation between self and faith that in Enlightenment ideology is endlessly coercive and unsatisfying.

The promise of the covenantal drama is the evocation of a community of joy that finds true communion and freedom in glad obedience. The entry point into such a community of joyful freedom in obedience is the practice of assertion and abandonment. It is this practice that our culture so fears and resists, that our community of faith has long understood to be the arena for obedience that glorifies God and makes the world a neighbor-hood. In such a practice both our *fearful conformity* and our *troubled autonomy* are overcome. Through such daring and constancy we become members of the Beloved Community.

3

Duty as Delight and Desire:
Preaching Obedience That Is Not Legalism

WE MAY AS WELL CONCEDE AT THE OUTSET THAT WE LIVE, ALL OF US, IN A promiscuous, self-indulgent society that prizes autonomy.[1] As a consequence, "obedience" is a tough notion, which we settle mostly either by the vaguest of generalizations, or by confining subject matter to those areas already agreed upon.

I

The fearfulness and avoidance of obedience, as conventionally understood among us, has in my judgment two root causes, both of which are alive and powerful, even though not often frontally articulated.

The first dimension of the problem is the Augustinian-Lutheran dichotomy of "grace and law," which runs very deep in Western theology. In his treatment of Paul, Augustine considerably upped the stakes of the issue in his crushing opposition to Pelagius, and Luther solidified that theological claim by boldly inserting the word "alone" in his reading of Paul, thus "grace *alone*." It is clear that by "law" Luther meant many different things, seemingly focused especially on life apart from the gospel. The result, however, has been a remarkable aversion to "works," as though obedience to the commands of God, that is, performances of "works," is in and of itself a denial of the gospel. Luther is of course much more subtle and knowing than this, but so he has been conventionally interpreted. The outcome has been a notion of gospel without demand, a notion that plays well in a "therapeutic" society.

An aspect of this strong dichotomy has been a latent but pervasive anti-Jewish stereotype. Thus "law" is easily assigned to the "Jews," and the Old Testament becomes a book of commandments that has been "superseded" by the free gospel of Christ. Such a common maneuver of course fails to understand the core dynamic of covenantal faith shared by Jews and Christians and inevitably feeds anti-Semitism.[2]

It is sufficient here simply to observe that such a reading of the gospel of Paul, powerfully reinforced by a sustained German-Lutheran reading of Romans, is at least open to question. Krister Stendahl has proposed that Augustine and Luther have massively misread Paul, who is concerned not with "guilt," but with Jewish-Christian relations in the early church.[3] And E. P. Sanders has contributed greatly to the exposition of Stendahl's proposal, so that this governing dichotomy needs to be seriously challenged and reconsidered.[4] The task of such reconsideration is a difficult one, given the force of these old categories.

The second dimension of our problem is the Enlightenment notion of unfettered freedom of "Man Come of Age." Indeed, the central program of the Enlightenment has been to slough off any larger authority to which obedience is owed, and that with special reference to the traditional authority of the church.[5] This notion of freedom is already rooted in Descartes' establishment of the *human* doubter as the norm of truth. Locke contributed to the cause with his notion of the human person as a rational, free decider, and Kant completed the "Turn Toward the Subject," in making the human autonomous actor the one who will shape functional reality. This Enlightenment ideology has received its popular form in a Freudian theory of repression in which human maturation is the process of emancipation from communal authority that is extrinsic to the individual person and therefore fundamentally alien to mature humanness. Thus the human goal is movement beyond any restraints that come under the category of repression.

It turns out, of course, that such a model of unfettered freedom is an unreachable mirage. The individual person is never so contextless, and in the end the fantasy of such freedom has culminated in the most choking of conformities.[6] There is, to be sure, an element of truth in Enlightenment models of liberation, but such a notion is almost always insufficiently dialectical to bear upon the actual human situation.

These theological-theoretical matters may seem quite remote from the concrete task of "preaching obedience." In my judgment, however, pastor and congregation must engage these powerful (even if hidden) categories and assumptions in critical and knowing ways, in order to face the commands of God honestly. The reason they must be faced is that they are concretely powerful, even if mostly unarticulated. It is false to take the "law/grace" dichotomy at face value, as though the creator of heaven and earth has no overriding, non-negotiable intention for God's creatures. It is equally false to accept the phony freedom of autonomy and find ourselves more deeply enmeshed in the commands of death. Only the exposure of these false articulations can permit the community of the gospel to discern and accept its true position before God, who loves, delivers, summons, and commands.[7]

II

A rereading of the gospel of grace and a reconsideration of Enlightenment ideology, in my judgment, will lead to a stunning and compelling fresh awareness: Our most serious relationships, including our relationship to the God of the gospel, are, at the same time, *profoundly unconditional* and *massively conditional*. One can, I submit, test this odd claim, both in terms of our normative theological materials and in terms of our lived experience.

Such a notion of course violates all of our either/or Aristotelian logic, but our most treasured relations are not subject to such an exclusionary logic.

Much Old Testament scholarship (including some of my own) has championed the notion that there are two traditions of covenant in the Old Testament, one unconditional (Abraham and David) and one conditional (Moses).[8] While this is critically correct, our theological task is to try to understand these textual claims taken all together.[9] The evidence to which I am drawn suggests in powerful ways that "conditional/unconditional" and "law/grace" are unworkable categories for understanding our most serious and treasured relationships. And these misguided polarities create great crises for understanding the odd dialectical character of the gospel.

We may take as emblematic of such relationships that are neither conditional nor unconditional, as do the Old Testament texts, the relations of husband-wife and parent-child. In either of these at its best, it is clear that the relationship is unconditional, that is, there is no circumstance under which the relationship will be voided. And yet in these very same relationships, there are high and insistent "expectations" of the other that shade over into demands.[10] And when these expectations are not met, there may be woundedness, alienation, or even rejection, even though the wounded party is powerfully committed.[11] The truth is that there is something inscrutable about such relationships that are both conditional or unconditional; or perhaps we should say neither unconditional nor conditional. If one seeks to make one term or the other final in characterizing such a relationship, we destroy the inscrutability that belongs to and defines the relationship.[12]

It may indeed be regarded as a far leap from our experience with such relationships as husband-wife and parent-child to our relation with God. It is of course a leap made artistically and boldly in the text itself. It will, moreover, be objected that one cannot reason by analogy or metaphor about God, and yet it is the only language we have for this most serious and freighted of all relationships. Moreover, we must ask why the poets of ancient Israel chose to speak this way about God. I suggest that such images are used because the poets who have given us our primal language for God are seeking a way to voice an inscrutability that overrides our logic and is more like the inscrutability of serious relationships than it is like anything else.[13]

The covenant God has with us, with Israel, with the world, is a command-premised relation. The covenant is based in command, and God expects to be obeyed.[14] There are, moreover, sanctions and consequences of disobedience that cannot be avoided, even as there are gifts and joys along with obedience.[15] The Torah is given for guidance, so that Israel (and all of Israel's belated heirs) are "clued in" to the defining expectations of this relationship. The Torah makes clear that the holy "Other" in this relationship is an Agent with will and purpose that must be taken seriously and cannot be disregarded or mocked.

Thus it is a *covenantal relation* that is the "underneath category" to which "grace and law," "conditional and unconditional" are subsets.[16] The "Other" in this relation is a real, live Other who initiates, shapes, watches over, and cares about the relation. The "Other" is both *mutual* with us and *incommensurate* with us, in a way not unlike a parent is mutual and incommensurate with a child, or a teacher is mutual and incommensurate with a student. This means that the relation is endlessly open, alive, giving and demanding, and at risk. This Holy Other may on occasion act in stunning mutuality, being with and for the second party, and so draw close in mercy and compassion, in suffering and forgiveness. It is, however, this same God who may exhibit God's self in unaccommodating incommensurability with rigorous expectation and dreadfulness, when expectations are not met. It is our desperate effort to reduce or "solve" the wonder of "the Holy one in our midst" that leads to such distortions as law and grace, freedom and servitude, unconditional and conditional.[17] No such pairing can adequately contain the inscrutability, liveliness, danger, and unsettled quality of this relationship. Israel thus knows that Torah is *guidance*, in order to be joyously "on the way," a way that constitutes the well-being of the relationship.[18]

III

This core insight about the richness of a covenantal relation still leaves for the preacher and the congregation the demanding work of taking seriously the specific commands of this covenantal "Other." Clearly the commands and guidance of the God of Israel and of the church are not vague and fuzzy, but quite concrete in how they concern the specificities of life. Those bound with this God are summoned to act differently in every sphere of life. Indeed, obedience consists in bringing every zone of our existence under the will, purpose, and expectation of this covenantal partner. While the concrete enactments of these commands in almost every case face ambiguity and complexity,[19] the most crucial issue for reflection and preaching is to frame the commands so that they are not alien impositions, extrinsic to our life, but belong to, and are embraced as, definitional for the very fabric of our existence.[20]

For that purpose, I suggest two possible interpretive strategies. The first is that the commands of God are the *disciplines essential to the revolution* that is Yahwism.[21] Every serious revolutionary movement requires exacting disciplines of its adherents. And while the requirements may vary, they all in substance concern single-minded devotion to the revolution, without any doubt, ambiguity, or reservation. A revolution has no chance of success unless all of its adherents are singularly committed to the vision and the project and are willing to play their assigned role with unquestioning reliability and responsiveness.

The revolution to which the biblical community is summoned is to enact in the world of social affairs a new practice of social relationships marked by justice, mercy, and peace, which touches all of life. In order to engage in such a practice, all those committed to this revolutionary vision are expected to enact the daily requirements concerning self toward God and self toward neighbor in order to "advance the revolution."

Or to change the figure slightly, Jesus and his disciples, that is, the ones under his discipline, are "on the way" as the "Kingdom of God draws near," a kingdom in which the "normalcies" of life are turned on their head. The disciples are variously summoned and dispatched to order their lives around "prayer and fasting," around empty-handed healing power, to live their lives as concrete testimony that the new realm is "at hand" and can be lived and practiced here and now.

In order to make this approach to "obedience" convincing, believers must come to see their baptism as entry into a new vision of reality, which carries with it all sorts of new possibilities that the world thinks impossible.[22] This vision of reality is an oddity in the world, at odds with all the conventional orderings of society—political, economic, and social. This "signing on" is not an "extra" added to a normal life, but entails a reordering of all of one's life from the ground up. The specificities of obedience must constantly be seen as derivative from, and in the service of, the larger revolution. It is clear that Moses imagined a whole new way of being in the world, a way ordered as covenant, and the commands of Sinai provide the guidance for that new way. And in like fashion, it is clear that the movement around Jesus evoked such hostility and resistance precisely because his movement subverted all conventional practices and forms in the world. No doubt such demands and disciplines became "legalistic" when the concrete requirement was no longer understood to derive from a larger revolutionary intention.

I am aware that such a notion of "revolutionary discipline" will not be easily compelling for most of us in excessively complacent establishment Christianity. I do imagine, however, that for many persons (especially young people), such a notion may indeed be a powerful attraction, for it is an enactment of a powerful hope for newness amid an increasingly failed and despairing society.

In any case, I suggest a second strategy for "preaching obedience." It is this: Believers are those who love God with their whole heart, or more colloquially for Christians, "love the Lord Jesus." Such "love" is to be understood in all its rich implication, both as *agape* and *eros*, as true heart's desire.[23] This is imagery not often utilized in our Calvinist inheritance, beset as we are with a heavy sense of duty. But alongside *duty*, in any serious relationship are *desire* and *delight*, the energetic will to be with the one loved, to please the one loved, to find in the joy of the one loved one's own true joy. Thus one in love is constantly asking in the most exaggerated way,

"What else can I do in order to delight the beloved?" In such a context, one does not count the cost, but anticipates that when the beloved is moved in joy, it will be one's own true joy as well. Indeed, in such a condition, one can find joy only in the joy of the beloved, and not apart from the joy of the beloved.

Thus the psalmist can speak of such true heart's desire:

> One thing I asked of the Lord,
>   that will I seek after:
> to live in the house of the Lord
>   all the days of my life,
> to behold the beauty of the Lord,
>   and to inquire in his temple. (Psalm 27:4)
> Whom have I in heaven but you?
>   And there is nothing on earth that I desire other than you.
>   (Psalm 73:25)

Of the last verse, Calvin comments:

> I know that thou by thyself, apart from every other object, art suf-
> ficient, yea, more than sufficient for me, and therefore I do not suf-
> fer myself to be carried away after a variety of desires, but rest in
> and am fully contented with thee. In short, that we may be satisfied
> with God alone, it is of importance for us to know the plentitude of
> the blessings which he offers for our acceptance.[24]

The true believer desires most of all being with the beloved.

None has understood this as well or as eloquently as Augustine, who saw that the most elemental craving of our life is communion with God. He begins his *Confessions* with the well-known affirmation:

> Thou awakest us to delight in Thy praise; for Thou madest us for
> Thyself, and our heart is restless, until it repose in Thee.[25]

And in his subsequent comment, he adds,

> Thou also gavest me to desire no more than Thou gavest.[26]

This sense of keen desire, not without its erotic dimension, is echoed in Bach's sterner notion of Jesus as the "joy of man's desiring." Thus "obedi-
ence" is a concrete, visible way of enacting and entering that desire, so that duty converges completely with the desire and delight of communion. It is not that obedience is instrumental and makes communion possible, but obedience itself is a mode of "being with" the desired in joy, delight, and well-being. In a quite concrete way, it is profoundly satisfying to do what the beloved most delights in.

Now I imagine that like "disciplines for revolution," the notion of "the desire of the beloved" will not be easy in the starchier traditions of Christian faith. Our more preferred strategy has been to renounce desire and focus on duty, on the affirmation that desire per se is an ignoble enterprise. This way of understanding obedience in relation to desire, however, honors the reality that we are indeed desiring creatures. God has made us so, and so we are. The work of obedience then, is not to squelch desire or deny it, as some modes of piety are wont to do, for then denied desire breaks out in destructive ways. Our work rather is to critique distorted desire and refocus desire on the true and faithful subject of our proper delight and longing. The intention of consumerism and its ideology of advertising is to distort and misdirect desire, as though the foundational desire of our life is for shoes, deodorant, beer, a car, or the best detergent. At the core of our crea-tureliness, however, such desires are fundamentally irrelevant. That is not what we want of life for they do not satisfy.

Faith confesses that it is none other than the very creator of heaven and earth who constitutes our true desire, so that only when our hearts rest in God can our restlessness be ended and satisfied. Thus the commandments are specific strategies for redirecting and reaffirming legitimate desire, not in any way a denial of desire, but in full affirmation of true desire. Thus God is the one for whom we seek, "as the deer longs for flowing streams" (Ps. 42:1). The metaphor suggests, according to the older translations, that the faithful "pant for" God and must have God for the wholeness of life. It is no wonder that obedience is a joy and delight, because it is an act in and of itself of communion with the one for whom we constantly and rightly yearn.

IV

The core summons to obedience, that is, (a) the core disciplines for the rev-olution, and (b) the core practices of our true desire, are voiced in the deca-logue.[27] As is well known, the two "tablets" of the ten commands are focused on "love of God" and "love of neighbor." On these two enterpris-es "hang all the Torah and the prophets." Such a simple prospectus for obe-dience comprehends enormous teaching material through which to invite the baptized to a new life of *revolutionary devotion* and *singleness of desire*.

The first four commands concerning "the love of God" reflect on the true subject of our life, the holy God who is our alpha and omega, the source and goal of all our life. This is the baseline for all biblical preaching and the primal claim of our faith. Our life consists in loving God for God's own sake. That is what we are created to do.[28]

How odd to yearn toward God! The commands in Exod. 20:1-7 assert that the primal quality and character of Yahweh deabsolutize every other claim and loyalty, and invite the renunciation of every addictive loyalty, conservative or liberal, which drives our life toward restlessness and phoni-ness. Moreover, the commands show that God is an "end" and not a "means," has no utilitarian value, but is to be loved purely for God's own sake. Such an affirmation about God cuts against all calculating obedience. Long before Job, Moses understood that Israel is called to "serve God for nought" (Job 1:9), that is, to gain nothing but only to be in this lively relation of duty and delight. Imagine what would happen if the church talked honestly about deabsolutizing all our quarrelsome addictions of mind and heart that tend to make all sorts of things absolutes that draw our life into knotted stomachs, clenched fists, and stern speech![29]

The second tablet (Exod. 20:8-17) asserts that the second true desire of our life, derivative from the first, is to have "good neighbors," that is, to live in a neighborhood. A true neighborhood is never a gift that floats down from the sky, but is wrought through the revolutionary work of obedience.[30] If we ever gain clarity about our true desire, it will quickly become evident to us that the yearning for good neighbors cannot be satisfied by any shoes, deodorant, beer, car, or detergent. They are not what we desire! And so our energy might be redirected toward neighborly matters like housing, education, health care, and away from coveting (Exod. 20:17) and all the distortions of commandments five through nine that serve coveting (Exod. 20:8-16). It is no wonder that the Decalogue is at the center of the Reformation catechisms, and that Luther and Calvin spent so much energy on them. Note well that when revolutionary vision and true desire are manifested, it becomes exceedingly difficult to be coercive and scolding about obedience. These commands are not primarily social restraints or modes of social control, but are about possibilities for life that emerge from "coming down where we ought to be." But conversely, when we have become ambivalent about the requirements of the revolution or caught in distorted desires, it is predictable that what begins as an offer of communion becomes coerciveness. And yet it is clear that no amount of reproof can help people find their way into true communion by way of revolutionary passion or focused desire. Such passion and desire are not generated by strident insistence or ideological imposition.

V

It is only slightly reductive to say that the two great accents of Freud and Marx, sexuality and economics, are the two great arenas for evangelical obedience, and the two zones in which we decide about our devotion to the covenantal revolution and where we enact our true desire. It follows that sexuality and economics, zones of great power, are also the most likely candidates for distortion and loss of the very communion for which we so yearn.

Freud understood that sexuality is a sphere of endless inscrutability, the arena of our true selves and the place in our life for deepest deception and pathology. Thus obedience in sexuality is a primary agenda of evangelical

faith, as is evident by the enormously destructive quarrels and high investment of energy in the church, after long centuries of repression, domination, and exploitation.

It is relatively easy (and I think useless) for the church simply to champion a flat "sex ethic" of a quite traditional kind. That of course is one very
live option in the church.[31] But if obedience in sexuality is to reflect and
derive from discipline for the revolution and/or a core desire for communion, then the categories of covenantal fidelity and covenantal freedom
must be primary ingredients in our thinking and acting. Such a perspective
requires much more than embracing traditional mores, because fidelity
means something quite different from "abstaining" or "staying married" or
"being straight." It means rather being in a relation that is genuinely life-
giving and life-receiving, where the work of neighbor regard is practiced.
And covenantal freedom means finding modes of fidelity congruent with
one's true self and the capacity to be emancipated from "legal" relationships that are in fact destructive and hopelessly demeaning. Thus the specificity of obedience in sexuality may most often come down to a "set of
workable conventions," but when that set of conventions is deeply coercive, it does not serve the covenantal revolution, and instead of focusing
true desire, it likely crushes desire or misdirects it, so that one's true self is
cut off from God and neighbor.[32]

Marx understood, conversely, that money is a sphere of endless
inscrutability, an arena of our true selves, and a place in our life for deep
deception and alienation. Obedience with money is a powerful agenda for
evangelical faith, as is evident by the profound disagreements in the church
about ways in which to think about the earning, saving, investing, sharing,
and spending of money, and the relative merits of different economic systems and policies. The Bible, moreover, spends enormous amounts of space
and energy on such issues.

It is relatively easy (and I think unhelpful) for the church to champion a
traditional ethics of money that simply reflects the practices of society,
whether in a market economy or a state economy. It is usual practice for the
church in our U.S. context to embrace what is conventionally understood as
"Protestant work ethic." It turns out, however, that such a "work ethic" is
for our time and place inordinately simplistic, and fails to take into account
the ambiguities and complexities of a global economic reality with astonishing disparities between "haves" and "have-nots."[33] Moreover, such an
ethic does not seem to make much contact with those who are so affluent
that they can create smaller zones of well-being that screen out the presence
of the neighbor.[34] It seems increasingly clear that the culminating command
of Moses, "Thou shalt not covet," now requires a carefully nuanced exposition that for affluent people moves well beyond such conventions as a
"tithe" and addresses the systemically driven acquisitiveness of a consumer
ethic in which neighbor questions have evaporated.[35]

As in sexuality, so in economics, covenantal obedience concerns the practice of covenantal fidelity and covenantal freedom, fidelity to see that all of our resources are held in trust in and for the neighbor with whom life is shared, and freedom that entails the practice of choices that attend both to the genuine regard of self and the genuine delight in generosity that enhances the neighborhood. True covenantal desire is not satisfied by acquisitiveness, even on a grand scale, but is satisfied only by the valuing of neighbor, even as self is valued. A reordered perception of obedience in economics is of enormous urgency for the covenantal revolution. It entails a repentance from false desire to which we have become blindly and uncritically committed.

It will be helpful, and in the end necessary, to see that obedience in sexuality and obedience in economics are of a piece. The interrelatedness of the two spheres of obedience exposes a profound contradiction in our common life in the U.S. It is conventional among us (and echoed by the more conservative voices of the church) to seek to impose puritanical restraint upon sexuality, all the while encouraging economic promiscuity for the sake of "economic growth."[36] It is not, however, a gain to reverse the process (with dissenting liberals in the church) to encourage economic transformation while being uncritically and thoughtlessly more open about liberty in sexuality. Either way, such disparity sends mixed signals and fails to maintain the delicacy of fidelity and freedom that belongs to covenantal relations.[37] Both coercive restraint and sanctioned promiscuity, whether in sexuality or in economics, violate the profound relatedness that belongs to evangelical obedience. The church must learn to speak differently about both spheres, in relation to each other, and in relation to the larger issues of genuine revolution and true desire.

VI

It is my judgment that we live in a moment in the U.S. church that requires a serious and explicit rethinking of the meaning of faithful obedience. At the core of evangelical faith is the claim that faith knows some things that matter for genuine life, which are now urgent for our society. Such an explicit rethinking that is the work of the whole congregation may operate with these affirmations:

1. The Enlightenment's offer of unfettered freedom without accountability is an unreachable mirage, an illusion never available to us.
2. The neat and conventional antithesis between law and grace is a distortion of faith, because there are no unconditional or conditional relationships in the gospel, but only relationships of fidelity that prize both freedom and accountability, the two always intertwined and to be negotiated.

3. Baptism is induction into the revolution of the coming rule of God. Like every revolution, this one has demanding disciplines that distinguish its adherents from all others.

4. Baptism is an acknowledgment of our true desire, our eagerness to be with, commune with, delight in, and delight through glad obedience to this life-giving holy Other.

5. It is precisely in our most primary zones of sexuality and economics that the demands and desires of this alternative life are most demanding and most satisfying. Those demands and desires consist not in the voiced demands of conventional morality nor in the self-indulgence that is an alternative to the flat demand, but in the struggle for the interface of freedom and faithfulness that requires endless interpretive work and reflection.

6. Rejection of disciplines of the revolution and the distortion of our true desire may take place either through flat, one-dimensional traditionalism or through self-indulgence. Such rejection and distortion constitute a betrayal of baptism and an attempt to live at least some of our life outside this coming rule and according to the rules of the kingdom of death.

7. Willingness to join the revolution or to practice this core desire can never be coerced. Such engagement is possible only by those who perceive their true identity in this coming rule. And then the disciplines and desire are winsome, joyous, and life-giving, not at all burdensome.

VII

In the core Mosaic proclamation of Deut. 6:5-6, immediately following the summons that Israel should listen (*shema*), Israel is told:

> You shall love the Lord your God with all your heart, and with all your soul, and with all your might. Keep these words that I am commanding you today in your heart.

Moses nicely juxtaposes *love* and *keep commandments*, because doing the will of the beloved is the way we enact love. Moreover, commandments are to be kept "in your heart," that is, they are not extrinsic, imposed, or coerced, but inhaled and embraced as one's own true will and intention.

This core summons is fleshed out in Deut. 13:4:

> The Lord your God you shall follow, him alone you shall fear, his commandment you shall keep, his voice you shall hear [*shema*], him you shall serve, to him you shall hold fast.

In this series of imperative verbs of obedience, two matters may be noticed. First, in Hebrew, in this English translation, the word order is inverted to give emphasis to the object of the verbs, "him . . . his . . . his . . . him." It is like a lover saying, "You, you, you."[38] Second, the last phrase, which the NRSV renders "hold fast" (*dabak*), is elsewhere "cleave" as in Gen. 2:24. It is a term of deep loyalty and devotion, a kind of personal, passionate attachment that far outruns any external, extrinsic rule. Moses envisions a relation of affectionate trust.

Finally, in Mark 10:17-22, Jesus does "pastoral care" for a person who seeks for "meaning" in his life. Jew that he is, Jesus responds to the man by asserting that the assurance he is seeking is found in full obedience to Israel's core commandments. Jesus assumes the man already knows the commandments. Beyond the commands, Jesus moves to "second level" obedience: "Go, sell what you own, and give the money to the poor . . . Come, follow me." It is as though the commandments are elemental, "first level" access to the revolution, but serious pastoral care moves to a more radical reorientation of life.

We observe three items in this narrative:

1. Jesus does not impose the commandments upon the man. The commands are not Jesus' idea. They are already there and already known at the beginning of the exchange. They are a premise of the conversation, to which Jesus can make appeal. Jesus credits the man with knowing them, so that there is not a cubit of coercion in the response Jesus makes to the man's serious enquiry. Nonetheless, the response of Jesus is indeed a serious one. A good future is to be shaped by what is known of who God is and what God desires.

2. Jesus loved the man (v. 21). Good pastoral care depends upon such a positive disposition toward the subject. Such love, however, does not lead to the romantic easiness of unconditional acceptance. It leads rather to truth-telling that concerns obedience. Nothing imposed, nothing harsh, nothing quarrelsome, only uncompromising truth-telling about the shape of well-being, spoken in love.

3. Jesus' love, plus the assumption of the commandments, led to a startling new demand, a demand too heavy for the questioner. The man decided not to join the revolution and decided to hold to his other "desire" of great possessions.

There is no anger or scolding in this meeting. We are not told that Jesus loved him any the less for his decision. But Jesus' love toward him, like that of Moses, is obedience-shaped. Jesus was clearly not much committed to "membership growth" in his little flock under revolutionary discipline. The difficulty, of course, is that truth-telling about well-being in a promiscuous society declares our common desires to be deathly. Obedience thus takes the form of alternative desire. When the Holy One is supremely desired, is the "joy of loving hearts," obedience becomes joy, and duty becomes delight. Such a claim is difficult in the midst of misperceived Enlightenment freedom and in distorted "free grace." But that in itself is no reason to doubt its life-giving truth.

Israel knew that obedience is the path to genuine life. The commands are a mode of God's grace:

> The law of the Lord is perfect,
>> reviving the soul;
> the decrees of the Lord are sure,
>> making wise the simple;
> the precepts of the Lord are right,
>> rejoicing the heart;
> the commandment of the Lord is clear,
>> enlightening the eyes;
> the fear of the Lord is pure,
>> enduring forever;
> the ordinances of the Lord are true
>> and righteous altogether.
> More to be desired are they than gold,[39]
>> even much fine gold;
> sweeter also than honey,
>> and drippings of the honeycomb.
>>> (Psalm 19:7-10)

4

Justice:
The Earthly Form of God's Holiness

FOR ALL OF OUR STUDY OF ARCHAEOLOGY AND HISTORY, WE UNDERSTAND almost nothing of the way ancient Israel bursts into our midst as a socio-economic-theological *novum*. Certainly that community has sociohistorical antecedents.[1] But it had no antecedent that adequately justifies its revolutionary appearance in public affairs. That revolutionary emergence of Israel is in part sociopolitical. Israel undertakes social practices and entertains social visions from its very inception that are radical in character, embracing an economics of sharing and a politics of equity. That sociopolitical dimension of reality is matched by the revolutionary character of Israel's God who, in important ways, shatters conventional notions of "godness" and begins with a "preferential option" for those who are to become Yahweh's special people in the world.

1

This revolutionary *novum* (newness of God, newness of public practices of power) is given us in the Exodus narrative that has become Israel's identifying narrative, mediated over time in "Passover imagination."[2] This narrative of Passover imagination (Exod. 1–15) provides for Israel the defining plot of Israel's historical drama with Yahweh, a drama that is repeatedly reenacted in many different times, places, and circumstances.

The key characters in the plot are three. *Israel* is first of all mindful of itself, its needs, its woundedness, its powerlessness, and its yearning for an alternative. Israel is ever again an exploited, oppressed community in need of an advocate and deliverer. Israel's antagonist is *Pharaoh*, the cipher in the Bible for every ruthless agent of exploitative power, the one eager to mobilize cheap labor for imperial aggrandizement. In the ongoing work of Passover imagination, Pharaoh becomes a type, who recurs in many guises in Israel's historical experience.

The third character in the drama, *Yahweh*, enters the plot abruptly and inexplicably. Yahweh appears in response to the voiced hurt and need of Israel (Exod. 2:23-25) and immediately takes on the role of deliverer. Yahweh's characteristic role is to stand over against Pharaoh, in order to champion Israel's cause with enough power and authority to legitimate Israel's life and to overturn oppressive structures, procedures, and assumptions. As the tale goes, Pharaoh eventually cannot withstand the resolve of Yahweh and, as a result, Israel escapes its oppressor, exercises freedom for its own life, and becomes "the subject of its own history."[3]

Through the process of tradition-building and liturgic reenactment, this narrative becomes the dominant plot for Israel's life, memory, hope, and ethics.[4] Israel's vision and practice of justice emerge in and from this narrative context. It is clear that justice as hoped for by Israel, resisted by Pharaoh, and finally given by Yahweh is not simply a retributive arrangement whereby each receives what is "deserved," but rather a radical notion of distributive practice that gives to each one what is needed—by way of legitimacy, dignity, power, and wherewithal—in order to live a life of well-being.[5] The subjects of this new justice of Yahweh make each a valued "end" of God, and not a "means" toward some other purpose. It is no wonder that this radical plot that conjoins theology and politics is thought by Michael Walzer to be the tap root and source of revolution everywhere in the Western world.[6] This Passover vision presents Yahweh, the creator of heaven and earth, as the active agent in the reshaping of human social power for the sake of human community and well-being. This tale tells of *Yahweh's* singular resolve, *Pharaoh's* inability to resist that resolve, and *Israel's* stunned, glad reception of a new possibility in the world.

II

While the Passover narrative energizes Israel's imagination toward justice, Israel's hard work of implementation of that imaginative scenario was done at "Mt. Sinai." I understand "Mt. Sinai" to refer to both (a) the initial covenant-making at Mt. Sinai (now lost to us as a historically recoverable event), and (b) the ongoing process of interpretation of Torah that persists in Jewish tradition as a way to keep the ancient commands of Sinai endlessly pertinent and compelling.

Moses' difficult work at Sinai is to transform the narrative vision of the Exodus into a sustainable social practice that has institutional staying-power, credibility, and authority. The most extreme understanding of Sinai is that Moses sought to fashion procedures, structures, and values to order a genuinely egalitarian community in which the political processes and economic resources of the community are made available for the sake of all members of the community, without reference to privilege or priority.[7] Against the elitism of Egypt, which predictably ended in oppression, this egalitarianism intends to curb every such claim of privilege. We may identify three phases of activity that sought to solidify the social requirements of covenantal justice, that is, the practice of genuine neighborliness.

1. The Ten Commandments (Exod. 20:1-17) constitute an attempt to lay down policy lines that will preclude barbarianism and nihilism.[8] The first three commands (vv. 2-7) assert the holiness of Yahweh beyond every ideological attempt to harness Yahweh for utilitarian ends. The absoluteness of

Yahweh beyond every ideological effort serves to deabsolutize every would-be absolute socio-economic-political intention that is in principle idolatrous.[9] Thus to "love God" means to refuse every other ultimate love or loyalty. The last six commands (vv. 12-17) concern love of neighbor. "Love of neighbor" here implies nothing romantic, but hard-nosed disciplines concerning protection of and respect for the life-sphere of every neighbor, including those who have no power to defend themselves or access to advocate their own interest. These elemental guarantees serve to protect the weak from the strong. The juxtaposition of the first three commands on the holiness of God and the last six on justice for the neighbor show that God's holiness and neighbor love are of a piece in this revolutionary experiment in ancient Israel. Indeed, Israel has known from the beginning that love of God cannot be remote from love of neighbor (1 John 4:20), and that holiness and justice always come together.

At the center of this list of policy statements at Sinai stands the regulation of sabbath, perhaps Israel's most stunning counter-cultural notion of justice.[10] In this command Israel broke decisively from the Pharaonic system of production and consumption. Israel asserts that "rest" for self, for neighbor, and even for God is the goal and quintessence of life. Now this rest is not passivity, but the kind of "at-homeness" that precludes hostility, competition, avarice, and insecurity. The sabbath provision of ancient Israel anticipates a community of peace, well-being, and joy.[11] There could hardly be a bolder refutation of Pharaoh's brick quotas than in this sabbath principle.

2. Israel's "policy statements" concerning an alternative mode of social relationships require specificity and implementation. The Ten Commandments, generalized as they are, wait to be interpreted and applied to local, specific circumstance.[12] In order to do that, "Moses" extrapolated from the commands, in part making use of already existing, non-Israelite materials. In enacting this inescapable interpretive move, it is clear that Israel's social vision was significantly compromised and toned down, in order to accommodate what we may call "social realism."

The earliest example of such interpretation toward specificity is in the "Covenant Code" of Exod. 21:1—23:19.[13] In this instruction, there are important articulations of Israel's radical social vision. Thus there is protection for the "resident alien" (Exod. 22:21-23; 23:9) and for the poor of Israel (Exod. 22:25-27), and a prohibition of bribes, which would bias justice toward the wealthy (23:6-8). These are extremely venturesome, concrete examples of a beginning in egalitarian justice. And in 21:2, the "sabbatic principle" is implemented, setting a limit on debt-slavery to which a neighbor can be held. This institution is a daring economic innovation. It is equally clear, however, that this Exodus version of justice was difficult to sustain in the face of vested interest, which most often shows up as property rights. Thus in the same law that protects Israelites and limits bondage for debt (21:2), Israel is willing to break up a family of the indebted for the sake of economic gain, for the creditor shall retain control of wife and children when the man is freed. Thus v. 4 adds a remarkably callused provision to the caring affirmation of v. 2. And in v. 26, the slave is said to be the "property" (*keseph*=silver) of the owner, showing that even in a less developed society, the disadvantaged can be made into commodities in the same way Hebrew slaves were treated as a commodity by Pharaoh.

This collection of laws makes clear that for Israel, its peculiar social vision was in endless struggle with its protection of vested interest and its enthrallment to ideological advantage.[14] This juxtaposition of vision and interest no doubt caused an ongoing interpretive dispute, as Israel sought at the same time to enact and to compromise its vision, which was kept available in its Passover liturgy. There is no doubt that such a radical vision will always keep such an interpretive struggle before this community, a struggle consisting of both theo-political and socioeconomic dimensions.

3. The book of Deuteronomy, commonly regarded as "Moses'" belated, mature, and covenantal interpretation of the demands of Sinai, evidences Israel's ongoing struggle for radical justice. We may mention only two points in that daring interpretive work. In 15:1-11, "Moses" elaborates on the "sabbatic provision" first surfaced in Exod. 21:2. In this more extended statement, so well exposited by Jeffries Hamilton, the instruction envisions a coming society "without the poor," who have been emancipated from their poverty.[15] Moreover, the intensity of infinitive absolutes in rhetoric of these verses provides for a complete economic rehabilitation of the bondservant. That is, the one with debts cancelled not only is returned to the "economy," but is entitled to and guaranteed the wherewithal to reenter the economy with dignity and viability. We may take this provision as the signature of Israel's notion of radical justice, advocating the responsibility of the creditor community for rehabilitation and restoration of those lost in the shuffle of economic transactions. Economics is understood as an instrument of a covenantal social fabric, and is not permitted to be a separate sphere with its own anti-neighbor procedures and laws.[16]

Second, Norbert Lohfink has observed that the provisions for institutional leadership of covenantal Israel in Deut. 16:18—18:22 concern a variety of "offices and authorities."[17] These include judge, king, priest, and prophet. Lohfink suggests that this material (which he regards as a "constitution") provides for the separation of powers as a check on any centralizing or oppressive absolutism.[18] Thus the polity of Israel, as well as its social vision, provides for covenantal procedures whereby the weak, powerless, and vulnerable are guaranteed structural protection. It is clear that for all of its compromise, this tradition of interpretation of the commandments retains much of the clarity and radicality of the Exodus. Israel's oddity in the world is not only because of its odd, justice-resolved God, but because of the social order envisioned, commanded, and legitimated by that God.

III

After the Torah traditions of Moses (Exodus and Sinai), the justice question pushes us to the prophets. Whatever may be the historical fact of relating Torah and the prophets, Israel's own canonical self-understanding is that the prophets are based in the Torah.[19] That is, the prophets continue to articulate, in the monarchial period and vis-à-vis the king, Israel's primal conviction that Yahweh's theological intention is the transformation of the socio-economic-political process. They intend that social structures and social relationships in Israel should be covenantal.

The corpus of the prophets, as it is now edited, is arranged with reference to the decisive debacle of 587 and the Babylonian destruction of Jerusalem in order to make two statements.[20] The two-fold editing of the prophetic books concerns first, the critical assertion that a community of unjust social relations will suffer the catastrophic judgment of Yahweh. That is, public affairs, including the incursions of the great powers into Israel, are understood by the prophets as an exercise of the sovereignty of Yahweh against a non-covenantal society. The prophets hold to a "metahistory" voiced in Israel's liturgy and memory, but not otherwise visible in the world.[21] In that metahistory, Yahweh continues to be a primary actor and Yahweh's decisive agenda concerns punishment for unjust social practices, that is, practices in Israel that replicate Pharonic policies.

The second element in "the final form of the text" is that Yahweh takes an initiative in permitting a new community to emerge after the debacle caused by injustice. This new community is empowered by Yahweh to make a fresh start in Torah obedience, whereby just social relations will be enacted and the community will be shaped according to the covenantal vision of Yahwism.

In the early (pre-exilic) prophets, we may mention two obvious examples of this process. Amos inveighs against a community that distorts justice and righteousness (5:7; 6:12) through bribery (5:12), self indulgence (6:4-6), and sharp business dealings (8:4-6).[22] At the very end of the pre-exilic period, when Jerusalem's public life ends in disaster, Jeremiah sounds the same themes. The prophet launches an assault against the exploiters who are "great and rich, fat and sleek," and who have such social advantage because,

> they know no limits in deeds of wickedness;
>> they do not judge with justice
>>> the cause of the orphan, to make it prosper,
>> and they do not defend the rights of the needy. (5:28)

More specifically, Jeremiah indicts the royal leadership of Jerusalem for its exploitative social policies (22:12-14), policies that are deeply in violation of care for the poor, which is the cornerstone of effective royal policy (cf.

Psalm 72:2-4). Thus the "unrighteousness" and "injustice" of the king is contrasted with that of his father Josiah:

> Did not your father eat and drink
>> and do justice and righteousness?
> Then it was well with him.
>> He judged the cause of the poor and needy;
> then it was well.
>> Is not this to know me? says the Lord. (Jer. 22:15-16)[23]

The entire sequence of prophets in the pre-exilic period represents an astonishing literary corpus that in some form surely reflects a staggering social movement.[24] This profound and demanding social criticism is an ongoing counterpart to the monarchy, for the monarchy entails social stratification, surplus value, and monopoly of privilege, all matters that create social inequity and exploitation. This conduct of kingship is not at all unusual or remarkable, for it is so in every developed society.

What is unusual and remarkable is this sustained social exposé and criticism by the prophets, which has a concrete policy edge to it, but which claims to be (and to some extent is accepted as) a transcendent voice of holiness. That voice, which will not be driven from the midst of Israel's social practice, insists that there is no wealth, power, knowledge, or privilege that can make a society safe, when the most elemental requirements of neighborliness are disregarded. The lyrical, imaginative poetry of the prophets is thrown in the face of exploitative social power with all the legitimacy of holiness.[25] Israel knows, moreover, that it must host this voice that cannot finally be silenced or banished from its arena of neighbor relations.

Oddly enough, in the present form, even these pre-exilic prophets so focused on Israel's destruction do not finish before they speak their alternative vision of a new society that will arise out of the debacle by the authority of Yahweh. Thus in 9:11-15, Amos envisions a new community of prosperity, security, order, and well-being. Even more extensively, Jeremiah envisions a reordered community of well-being in which there is fertility and prosperity, and the resumption of dance, joy, comfort, and bounty (31:12-14). As the cessation of communal rituals of joy marked a terrible ending of social process (cf. Jer. 7:34, 16:9, 25:10), so now the resumption of such rituals signals the rehabilitation of a community of well-being:

> There shall once more be heard the voice of mirth and the voice of gladness, the voice of the bridegroom and the voice of the bride, the voices of those who sing, as they bring thank offerings to the house of the Lord:
> "Give thanks to the Lord of hosts,
>> for the Lord is good,
>> for his steadfast love endures forever!" (Jer. 33:10-11)

This same accent on justice is unabated in some of the voices of prophecy in the exile and after the exile, that is, after the nullification of the monarchy. In the later materials of the book of Isaiah, addressed to Israel in a forlorn condition, the enigmatic figure of the prophet is identified as one sent for the sake of justice:

> Here is my servant, whom I uphold,
>   my chosen, in whom my soul delights;
> I have put my spirit upon him;
>   he will bring forth *justice* to the nations . . .
>   he will faithfully bring forth *justice*.
> He will not grow faint or be crushed
>   until he has established *justice* in the earth;
> and the coastlands wait for his teaching. (Isa. 42:1-4)

If we take "the servant" to be Israel, then Israel's vocation, even in its marginalized situation of exile, is nonetheless to "establish justice," the very same justice around which Moses organized his anti-hegemonic revolution, and to which Amos harshly summoned Israel. That mandate for justice is reiterated in late Isaiah as a thematic summons to justice (56:1), as a call to inclusiveness (56:2-8), as a vocation of communal responsibility for the needy (58:6-9), and as an "impossible possibility" for the new creation given by God (65:17-25).

The lyrical imagination of later Isaiah is matched by the resolve of Yahweh, according to Ezek. 34:11-16 and in the utterance of Zechariah. This accent in a later priestly prophet is all the more astonishing, because Zechariah, along with Haggai, is commonly understood in terms of temple building and long-term hope. Zechariah, however, clearly stands in this same relentless justice tradition of Israel and so can never move far away from a Mosaic cadence that comes to be characteristic in Israel:

> Thus says the Lord of hosts: Render true judgments, show kindness
> and mercy to one another; do not oppress the widow, the orphan,
> the alien, or the poor; and do not devise evil in your hearts against
> one another. (Zech. 7:9-10)

In season and out of season, Israel holds to this vocation. The prophetic urgings of later Isaiah, Ezekiel, and Zechariah finally come to quite concrete effect in the reforming activity of Nehemiah. While the Ezra-Nehemiah effort is commonly seen to be concerned with the rebuilding of the city and the recovery of the Torah, it is clear that neighborliness as an economic-political necessity is on their horizon. In Nehemiah 5, the great "urban planner" of ancient Israel requires an economic reform whereby the "haves" and "have nots" must act together in Yahwistic good faith. This is again the "sabbatic principle" at work, redefining social relationships:

> Restore to them, this very day, their fields, their vineyards, their
> olive orchards, and their houses, and the interest on money, grain,
> wine, and oil that you have been exacting from them. (Neh. 5:11)

This appeal, which is reported to be effectively implemented, is a concrete
outcome of this long tradition of holiness evident in social relations as justice.

IV

The public utterance of justice in the prophetic oracles and the (occasional)
practice of public justice are fully reflected in the texts we have mentioned.
That public possibility in Israel expressed in Torah and prophets, however,
is matched and sustained by the liturgical-pastoral tradition of the Psalter.
That is, justice not only is a public issue, but permeates Israel's life of devotion, piety, spirituality, and prayer.[26] Justice is what Israel pondered as it
entered into God's own presence.

In the great doxological liturgies of Israel, Yahweh is affirmed as a doer
of justice, the very kind of justice toward the oppressed and marginated
that Pharaoh could never host or imagine:

> Mighty King, *lover of justice*,
>   you have established equity;
> you have executed justice
>   and righteousness in Jacob. (Ps. 99:4)[27]

The very character of Yahweh is understood under the rubric of justice in
quite specific ways. This is a God

> who executes justice for the oppressed;
> who gives food to the hungry.
> The Lord sets the prisoners free;
>   The Lord opens the eyes of the blind.
> The Lord lifts up those who are bowed down;
>   The Lord loves the righteous.
> The Lord watches over the strangers;
>   he upholds the orphan and the widow,
> but the way of the wicked he brings to ruin. (Ps. 146:7-9)

Justice is no extra for Yahwism, but is at the core of Yahweh's own identity, so that this community cannot have Yahweh as God without this public
agenda.

As Israel's hymns celebrate who Yahweh is and what Yahweh does, the
complaint psalms regularly address Yahweh in the imperative, urging that
God act and intervene in order to transform situations of exploitation and
injustice:[28]

> Rise up, O Lord; O God, lift up your hand;
>   do not forget the oppressed. (Ps. 10:12)

> For we sink down to the dust;
> > our bodies cling to the ground.
> Rise up, come to our help.
> > Redeem us for the sake of your steadfast love. (Ps. 44:25-26)
> Give justice to the weak and the orphan;
> > maintain the right of the lowly and the destitute.
> Rescue the weak and the needy;
> > deliver them from the hand of the wicked . . . .
> Rise up, O God, judge the earth;
> > for all the nations belong to you! (Ps. 82:3-4, 8)[29]
> Rise up, O judge of the earth;
> > give to the proud what they deserve! (Ps. 94:2)

As the hymns proclaim Yahweh's commitment to justice, so the laments hold Yahweh to that commitment, anticipating that Yahweh's deep resolve is to transform the world into a genuine community of neighbors.

That sustained reflection upon the character of Yahweh in hymn and lament issues, in the Psalter, into ethical reflection. That is, what Yahweh wills and does in the world is echoed and replicated by the adherents of Yahweh. Thus those who "fear Yahweh" and "delight greatly in Yahweh's commandment" act in certain ways (Ps. 112:1):

> They rise in the darkness as a light for the upright;
> > they are gracious, merciful, and righteous.
> It is well with those who deal generously and lend,
> > who conduct their affairs with justice . . .
> They have distributed freely,
> > they have given to the poor;
> their righteousness endures forever;
> > their horn is exalted in honor. (Ps. 112:4-5, 9)

Human conduct that enacts justice is a counterpart to Yahweh's own work of justice.[30] For that reason, Israel's worship life has an ethic of justice at its core and never imagines being in God's presence except as those who have justice as their identifying agenda (cf. Pss. 15, 24).

Indeed, in the "final form of the text," Psalms is reckoned as a corpus of Torah piety.[31] That is, Psalm 1 sets the tone for the entire Psalter. Those who worship and trust Yahweh and who appeal to Yahweh "meditate day and night upon the Torah," which, according to the tradition of Moses, is a mandate for revolutionary, transformative justice in the world. In its positive aspects, Torah activity transforms the neighborhood. In its negative function, the Torah refuses the anti-neighborly ways of the world that can only end in brutality and nihilism. Thus the characteristic Israelite of Torah piety seeks God's goodness and trusts in God's commands for justice:

> I know, O Lord, that your judgments are right,
>> and that in faithfulness you have humbled me . . . .
> You are righteous, O Lord,
>> and your judgments are right. (Ps. 119:75, 137)

V

It is our insistence that this revolutionary eruption of justice in the world in the life of Israel is a primal motif in many varieties and genres of texts, including the Exodus narrative of liberation, the commands of Sinai and its interpretive after-life, the prophetic oracles, and the meditative piety of the Psalter. Before we finish, however, we must add a qualifying note of candid realism. The transformative agenda of justice is not everywhere uncontested in the texts of ancient Israel. This visionary intentionality, with such radical practical implications, always lives in the presence of uncompromising "realism," which bespeaks ideology, vested interest, and pragmatism. Not only is there a *transformative* notion of justice, but there is alongside it a justice that intends to *maintain* the status quo and to protect present power arrangements with all of its several advantages and disadvantages.[32]

This countertheme of pragmatism that resists excessive visionary intentionality is found in many places in the text, but in none is it more visible and sustained than in the wisdom instruction of the book of Proverbs. Issues of "wealth and poverty" in the book of Proverbs are characteristically understood so that the prosperous understand themselves as the righteous who deserve generous blessings and who have no call to share with the "undeserving poor."[33] Thus, for example,

> A slack hand causes poverty,
>> but the hand of the diligent makes rich. (Prov. 10:4)
> A generous person will be enriched,
>> and the one who gives water will get water. (Prov. 11:25)
> Poverty and disgrace are for the one who ignores instruction,
>> but one who heeds reproof is honored.(Prov. 13:18)

The outcome of such an understanding of the shape of reality is self-congratulations. The root of such a view, however, is the theological claim that this is a tightly reliable world in which there is no slippage between goodness and blessing and therefore between "badness" and disadvantage. It is this close, uncritical view of things that the friends of Job state in the most blatant, exaggerated form.[34]

It is not possible here to engage in an extended critique of this "ethic of self-congratulations," which is at odds with Israel's more radical justice commitment. It is enough to notice that this latter view is also "biblical" and like the more radical view of justice, it is rooted in actual social experience and thought by its adherents to be a legitimated form of Yahwism.

The result of this tension between a *tradition of revolutionary transformation* and a *tradition of maintenance of the status quo* is to see that Israel endlessly faced a disputatious conversation about justice. This conversation is always an adjudication of vision and experience (sometimes the experience of deprivation and sometimes the experience of privilege). That disputatious conversation in which the community of faith must be engaged includes disputes about the character of God, the ethical mandate for the faithful, and the public policy possibilities that flow from decisions about the character of God and the ethical mandate for the faithful. That conversation cannot ever, in the historical process, be fully resolved. There can be, at the most, provisional settlements made in particular conversations. Those provisional settlements, however, are endlessly reopened in new circumstances and fresh contexts. What is certain is that the heirs of this textual tradition are heirs to this difficult conversation and must continue such difficult and conflictual reflection.

As one of the heirs of the ancient textual tradition of Judaism, the New Testament community, which sought to understand the "news" of Jesus in light of this textual inheritance, could not escape the same issues.

5

The Cunning Little Secret of Certitude: On the First Great Commandment

The issues facing the church are broad and deep and concern all Christians and all churches in the U.S. culture. They are not the private property nor the special burden of any one tradition, and therefore we must all think about them long and together. My responsibility is not that I should say something new to you, but that I should think with you yet again about the things we have known longest and trusted most deeply.

1

You know how the story goes in the Old Testament. It aims, from the outset, at *Sinai*. That is where the story is headed. It arrives there in a sweep that is large and wondrous, a recital of defining miracles that give life upon which we dare not presume and that we dare never forget.

At the outset there is *chaos*. That is where the story begins:

> The earth was a formless void and darkness covered the face of the deep. (Gen. 1:2)

The disorder is deep, elemental, and primordial, long extant before we arrived there with our mothers and fathers; they, moreover, had no great curiosity about the origin of chaos, but they saw it clearly and knew it well. God said, "Let there be light." Then God said, "Be fruitful and multiply, and subdue it." Then God said, "It is very good." And God rested. We treasure the move from chaos to good creation, and we know the name of the creator.

At the outset of the story of our mothers and fathers, there was *barrenness*. In that patriarchal, land-hungry community, barrenness is not only a shame and a disgrace, regularly blamed on the women. After shame and blame, it means no patrimony, no heir, no future. And the long tale reiterates the crisis, seemingly without end:

> Now Sarah was barren; she had no child. (11:30)
> Isaac prayed to the Lord for his wife, because she was barren. (25:21)
> But Rachel was barren. . . . she bore . . . no children. . . . she said . . . "Give me children, or I shall die." (29:31—30:1)

All these mothers in this family of promise, deeply set in the promise to "be fruitful and multiply," all without hope.

And then, inscrutably, against circumstance, in fidelity, we are told:

> The LORD did to Sarah as he had promised. . . . Now Sarah said,
> "God has brought laughter for me; everyone who hears will laugh
> with me." (21:1, 6)

She laughed in joy. And after her Rebekah and Rachel and Elizabeth and all
our mothers have laughed the Easter laugh, barren to birth, sorrow to joy,
despair to hope.

At the outset, in Egypt, "the Egyptians treated us harshly," were endlessly ruthless and exploitative, and we knew about *slavery.* Our mothers
and fathers cried out,

> They groaned under slavery and cried out. (Exod. 2:23)

They could do nothing else in their oppression, not even able to address
their cry to anyone. But we are told:

> Out of the slavery their cry for help rose up to God. God heard their
> groaning, and God remembered his covenant with Abraham, Isaac,
> and Jacob. God looked upon the Israelites, and God took notice of
> them. (vv. 23-25)

And then a process of confrontation, negotiation, bargaining, and the slow
availability of the God of Israel, until finally we are told:

> Then the prophet Miriam, Aaron's sister, took a tambourine in her
> hand; and all the women went out after her with tambourines and
> with dancing. And Miriam sang to them:
>   "Sing to the Lord, for he has triumphed gloriously;
>   horse and rider he has thrown into the sea." (15:20-21)

Miriam and all her sisters danced the dance of new life, when bondage had
turned to freedom and oppression had become the inexplicable gift of liberation.

At the outset of the wilderness, just out beyond Egypt, they had thought
en route to the good land of promise, but by day one, they noticed . . . no
food:

> If only we had died by the hand of the Lord in the land of Egypt,
> when we sat by the fleshpots and ate our fill of bread; for you have
> brought us out into this wilderness to kill this whole assembly with
> hunger. (Exod. 16:3)

The hunger was deep and massive, no resources. And then, beyond expectation, the creator of heaven and earth gave bread from heaven to our
mothers and fathers on earth:

> In the morning there was a layer of dew around the camp. When the
> layer of dew lifted, there on the surface of the wilderness was a fine

flaky substance, as fine as frost on the ground. When the Israelites saw it, they said to one another, "What is it?" For they did not know what it was. Moses said to them, "It is the bread that the Lord has given you to eat. This is what the Lord has commanded: 'Gather as much of it as each of you needs, an omer to a person according to the number of persons, all providing for those in their own tents.'" The Israelites did so, some gathering more, some less. But when they measured it with an omer, those who gathered much had nothing over, and those who gathered little had no shortage; they gathered as much as each of them needed. (16:13b-18)

They learned, against their expectation, that the wilderness is governed by God, a place of nourishment and protection.

The Bible moves through these dramatic acts, perhaps in concentric circles, beginning in the cosmic drama of chaos and creation and finally coming down to a simple loaf of bread for our mothers and fathers who learned to pray daily for bread:
• chaos to creation,
• barrenness to birth,
• oppression to liberation,
• hunger to bread.

It is the story of our life. It is an incredible narrative in which we are deeply and firmly set, the God of generosity who overrides every needful circumstance by miracle. We have been retelling this to our daughters and sons forever, even as our fathers and mothers have recruited us into this odd account of reality. The tales told in this sequence of miracles evoke a community of buoyancy and exuberance and energy and gratitude. That's us!!

II

And then we arrived at Sinai. The Israelites put the story together for us, so that it all moves toward Sinai. As you know, Sinai takes up half the Pentateuch and, in the end, it is the work of Sinai that creates a people of special intentionality. It is at Sinai that the Torah is given and Israel is formed and covenant is enacted. In these solemn, dense ceremonies, Israel is formed as a social experiment in the world, as an alternative society bent to enact a counter-vision of reality in the world. We say, moreover, that a deep line runs from Sinai to the church that is a "provisional demonstration" of what God will work in the world, soon or late.

This was a dangerous meeting, this moment of formation. Israel was invited to the mountain but at the same time Israel was warned not to get too close. There was smoke and fire, and trumpets and trembling, a preparation and context for what God would say. And now speaks the God,
• who orders creation out of chaos,
• who gives births to our barren mothers,

- who frees slaves from the brutality of slavery,
- who multiplies bread in the face of limitless hunger.

It is this God who speaks. You know what was said in that moment: "I am Yahweh!" I am the Lord.

> I am the LORD your God who brought you out of the land of Egypt,
> out of the house of slavery.

This is the God who presides over life-giving miracles:

> You shall have no other gods. (Exod. 20:1)

This is not monotheism, not speculative theology, not an argument about metaphysics. It is rather a direct, personal, immediate demand made by the God of all miracles. By this lean demand, our mothers and fathers are gathered to the miracle-worker and are set to live in the presence of the miracle-worker, and to respond to Yahweh's primal expectations. The demand is bald, unqualified, unadorned, unexplained, unjustified. Just me. Just you toward me. No extras. No qualifications, not any assurances.

And to make sure the demand is not misunderstood, two by-laws accompany the demand. No graven images:

> You shall not make for yourself an idol, whether in the form of any-
> thing that is in heaven above, or that is on the earth beneath, or that
> is in the water under the earth. You shall not bow down to them or
> worship them; for I the Lord your God am a jealous God, punish-
> ing children for the iniquity of parents, to the third and the fourth
> generation of those who reject me, but showing steadfast love to the
> thousandth generation of those who love me and keep my com-
> mandments. (vv. 4-6)

No form, no replication, no catching and solidifying, no domestication, no reduction. This is the same God who in the time of David declined a temple: free . . . free . . . free . . . holy . . . free . . . dangerous . . . free . . . unencumbered . . . free.

By-law number two:

> You shall not make wrongful use of the name of the Lord your God,
> for the Lord will not acquit anyone who misuses his name. (v. 7)

Our easy piety has taken this command too long to mean: do not swear, do not curse, do not use obscenity or vulgarity. These rules of civility are surely good ones; but they are not the point of the command. The point, rather, is that the deep power of Yahweh, Yahweh's name, Yahweh's authority, Yahweh's recognition, Yahweh's claim, cannot be harnessed or employed or utilized or mobilized for lesser human projects, even good human projects, like stewardship or prayer or building programs or morality or national security or war—because God has no utilitarian value and will not be used.

The God of Sinai is not to be recruited or associated with our best projects, liberal or conservative.

The three commands together bespeak an unapproachable holiness that puts God beyond us and out of reach. And Israel's role—our role—is to be addressed, to listen, to hear, to answer, the entire transaction caught in the term *shema* that we weakly translate "obey." That is, this God will be obeyed, will address, will have us attend, in order to yield, to answer, to resonate with, to be available as willing subject of this holy God.

The miracles of creation-birth-liberation-bread end in *obedience*, hearing and answering. Abraham Heschel, great rabbi and teacher of us all, has written:

> To be is to obey. . . . The transcendence of being is commandment, being here and now is obedience. . . . To be is to obey the commandment of creation. . . . What is endures as a response to a command. . . . Being is obedience, a response. "Thou art" precedes "I am." I am because I am called upon to be. . . . Living involves acceptance of meaning, obedience, and commitment.[1]

And before Heschel, John Calvin had said it right and well:

> There also emerges the beginning of true understanding when we reverently embrace what it pleases God there to witness of himself. But not only faith, perfect and in every way complete, but all right knowledge of God is born of obedience.[2]

And in our own time, Cynthia Ozick, probing the costliness of this God, asserts:

> The ornamental elegance of the King James Version gives us the Ten Commandments with a rather baroque thrill to them—all those Thou Shalt Not's. But if you listen to the Commandments in Hebrew, you will hear a no-nonsense abruptness, a rapidity and a terseness. They begin with Lo, the Hebrew word for No. . . . The Torah the Jews carry stands for No, for all the things we ordinary mortals want to do and take glee in doing.[3]

Jews and Christians are agreed about the primacy and centrality of obedience. It is our splendor to respond to the will of God, and it is—as we evidence among us—our great problem. Midst the splendor and the problem, it is crucial for us to remember that it is the creator over chaos, the giver of birth in the face of barrenness, the liberator from slavery, the giver of wilderness bread who bids us *shema*.

III

Our mothers and fathers have long pondered the first commandment with its two provisos:

- Already in Deuteronomy, Moses had explicated the commandment:

> You shall love the Lord your God with all your heart, and with all your soul, and with all your might. Keep these words that I am commanding you today in your heart. Recite them to your children and talk about them when you are at home and when you are away, when you lie down and when you rise. (Deut. 6:5-7)

- Hosea, midst an ocean of compromising syncretism, had seen the urgency of the command:

> Yet I have been the Lord your God
> ever since the land of Egypt;
> you know no God but me,
> and besides me there is no savior. (Hos. 13:4)

He had, moreover, seen that the demand has immense dangers when it is neglected:

> I will fall upon them like a bear robbed of her cubs,
> and will tear open the covering of their heart;
> there I will devour them like a lion,
> as a wild animal would mangle them.
> I will destroy you, O Israel;
> who can help you? (Hos. 13:8-9)

- Isaiah in exile has turned the sweeping claim of Yahweh to the huge benefit of Israel:

> For my name's sake I defer my anger,
> for the sake of my praise I restrain it for you,
> so that I may not cut you off.
> See, I have refined you, but not like silver;
> I have tested you in the furnace of adversity.
> For my own sake, for my own sake, I do it,
> for why should my name be profaned?
> My glory I will not give to another.
> Listen to me, O Jacob,
> and Israel, whom I called:
> I am He; I am the first,
> and I am the last. (Isa. 48:9-12)

- Jesus engaged in rabbinic dispute, the kind we engage in when we trade arguments about our favorite commandments:

> Which commandment is the first of all? (Mark 12:28)

He answers without pause:

> The first is, "Hear O Israel: the Lord our God, the Lord is
> one; you shall love the Lord your God with all your heart,
> and with all your soul, and with all your mind, and with all
> your strength." (vv. 29-30)

The terse prohibition of Sinai has become the love commandment that
sets God alone above all else, to be regarded with the loyalty of our entire
being. The command to love God may be taken, as may be inevitable in our
society, as an *affective* matter, to be "in love" with God—except it is difficult to imagine this God being huggable. Or alternatively, the command
may be taken, as Old Testament scholars mostly think, in *political* idiom, as
treaty language concerning a pledge to the policies of Yahweh. Either way,
as affective or as political, the terse command of Yahweh bespeaks radical,
singular, undivided attentiveness to the one who miraculously orders and
reorders life in wholeness and well-being.

Israel in every generation and circumstance is invited to other loyalties—
political, economic, religious, and moral. And of course it is not different in
every circumstance and generation of the church. And in every such circumstance, we are drawn by memory and instruction and liturgy and exe-
gesis back to Sinai, to the vision of the holiness that dwells at the center of
our peculiar imagination.

IV

Now I make a big textual maneuver that you must grant me. I have been
speaking of the core of the Torah tradition. I turn our attention now to the
Psalter, to the intimacy and detail and routine of Israel's worship. For it is
in the worship of our community that the sweeping claims of Torah are
processed with pastoral simplicity and directness and candor. Israel knows
the Torah well; but knowing the Torah well, it must find ways to live its life.
There are in the Psalter, as you know, the great hymns of faith that in grand
innocence and without embarrassment sound the deep claims of Sinai, the
rhetoric that continues to dominate our hymnals. And there is a strong
body of complaints and laments that speak to God in hopeful candor when
things are amiss, a candor mostly in short supply in our triumphal tradition. But I have chosen to speak not of the hymns or complaints, but of two
reflective psalms in which we can see and have modeled a processing of
faith in which the large claims of Torah must be handled, so to say, "on the
ground," in the midst of real life.

I will tell you why I have chosen these two psalms against the backdrop
of Torah. It is because these psalms in their reflectiveness indicate the delicacy of real life in faith, the ambivalence that must be processed and offered
to God, and the courage required to live honestly before God from whom
no secret can be hid and who mandates and compels uncompromising love.

I listen to the *loud certitudes* of church people of the right and of the left about sexuality and economic justice. And I also have my own set of certitudes that in unguarded moments are loud. But I discern something else as well. I notice among the genuinely pious—who may be intermittently loud—a wonderment, a bewilderment, a hopefulness that does not admit of easy loudness. We may call it diffidence or ambivalence. The great anthropologist, Victor Turner, called it *liminality*. By the term Turner means an in-between state in which old configurations of power and certitude are gone, but there is as yet no new configuration that is visible or generally accepted. Liminality is not a comfortable state for a society, nor for a church. But it does come upon us; moreover, my impression is that liminality is an occasion of openness when newness may happen, or as we say theologically, liminality is a situation of immense openness to the newness of the Spirit. It has occurred to me:

1. that our situation in the church now is one of liminality in which old configurations of power and certitude are increasingly seen to be inadequate, and new configurations are not yet evident, a place in which the spirit may work newness and

2. that these reflective psalms evidence precisely such a posture of faith in liminality.

I focus this way because it is my urging that folk like us may declare a sabbath from loud certitudes and notice the high degree of liminality that is among us where God is at work. It is my impression that loud certitude may indeed be an enemy of the newness that God is seeking to give us. And therefore, possibly, these reflective psalms may be our best texts just now. After all, if one knows, we need not reflect or host ambiguity. So let me try.

I have selected two psalms, one of which is not so much used among us, and one that is much used among us, but only in some of its parts. I have taken these two psalms, against a backdrop of the Great Commandment, to focus on what I regard as two seductions much at work among us, seductions that I think are often not either/or, not one or the other, but both at the same time.

First *Psalm 73* and the *secular* seduction. This psalm is a reflective one in which the speaker tells the tale of a personal religious crisis. I read it with you to suggest it may be a map for our common struggle just now to be the church. I call it *the temptation to autonomy*, a kind of lip-service faith in which God may be an ornament but no real factor.

1. Verse 1 is the premise of the poem, a premise perhaps derived from old Torah commands. Moses had taught that people who keep the commandments will be blessed. Job's friends had certainly believed it and had told Job as much, and now that confident moral claim upon God is voiced:

> Truly God is good to the upright,
> > to those who are pure in heart. (v. 1)

God is good, but not to everyone. God is peculiarly, unreservedly, and attentively good to the upright, to the Torah keepers, to the ones who love God with everything without reservation. It is a simple moral calculus at the heart of the Bible. The two lines of the verse are fully parallel. Except you may notice that most English translations say:

> Truly God is good to Israel.

You can take it either way, Israel or *yasarel* ("to the upright"). The second line makes it plain. It is the kind of innocence into which we induct our children. It is the keynote of Psalm 1 through which the Psalter is to be read and understood:

> Blessed are those who do not walk in the way of the wicked . . . for
> the Lord watches over the way of the righteous. (Ps. 1:1, 6)

2. That simple, innocent affirmation of trust in the goodness of God, however, is not easy to sustain. And so in vv. 2-16, the first large body of the text, the psalmist describes a crisis in that simple teaching, a crisis that I suppose comes to any noticing member of the community. The psalmist admits—out loud—that he just about stumbled out of the covenantal calculus. He watched the arrogant rich. He noticed wheeler-dealers who had no compunction and who worked the mechanism of free market consumerism to their advantage. He noticed them and he envied them (vv. 2-3).

These are people who have strayed outside the moral containment of v. 1 and have gotten on very well. They have no trouble and no pain. They are sleek, well-fed, the hair dresser twice a week, nattily dressed in best fashion, just back from Florida with a beautiful tan. Their pride and self-confidence is much exhibited, and they practice violence and exploitation of the poor without any second thoughts. They understand the leverage of power and access and know how to manipulate. They have endless parties, are seen at all the best places, irreverent, free, self-indulgent, narcissistic, much admired, on the make, filling the gossip columns with their last exotic venture. I am not making this up; it is in the psalm (vv. 4-8).

They regard religion as stuffy, pompous coercion and will not fool with it. They proceed in walk and in talk as though there were no God, no moral limits, nothing sacred (vv. 8-9). And the worst is their celebrity status (v. 10)! Conclusion:

> All in vain I have kept my heart clean
> and washed my hands in innocence. (v. 13)

Who speaks here? Well, it could be a pastor who earns one-third or one-fourth as much as the big folks in the parish. Or it could be somebody with an acute social conscience, somebody who cares a lot and works for the needy and on most days it all seems faithful. But the psalm comes from an odd day when with a sinking feeling you wonder if it is all worth it. You decide in a despising, self-pitying moment that it is all an illusion and you think to join them, because it works better for them. And some depart to join them. Some pastors become cynical and exploitative. Some churches become cunning and operate like the Kiwanis or the American Legion, and some seminary professors and denominational executives get so used to a handsome salary that the old costs of faith seem like out-moded superstitions.

What is going on is chipping away at the first commandment. A few compromises with other loves. A few domestications of God, a rendezvous with an image or an idol that looks a little like free-market success. A little compromise and God's name (in vain) serves well-being and the church becomes so accommodated that the command to love only God is softened and relaxed and nullified. And we ourselves become the key players, in which faith is promotion and discipleship dissolves into massive ego. It is a temptation because God's goodness, contrary to v. 1, is distributed indiscriminately, so who cares?! It is the *certitude of the liberated agent* who gets very pragmatic.

3. It happens. It almost happened to this psalmist. But not quite (vv. 15-17)! Because at the last minute, in the eleventh hour of fateful sell-out to self-indulgence, the psalmist is brought up short and does not want to be remembered in that way (v. 15). The psalmist is completely bewildered by the theodicy question about virtue going unrewarded (v. 16).

Until . . . get this—*until* big time:

> Until I went into the sanctuary of God. (v. 17)

The speaker regroups and refocuses and goes into the sanctuary, into the old Torah tradition, into the mystery of sacramental life, into the tabernacle, before the mercy seat, into the very presence of God. His envy and compromise and self-indulgence are checked by the Holy Mystery. In that holy mystery, saturated with Torah memory, the psalmist receives a second, revised version of reality. Verse 17, I suggest, is a liminal moment when things could have gone either way. The speaker is open and ambivalent, having voiced the torture of ambiguity.

4. In that daunting moment, the speaker retreats from *secular autonomy* and reperceives everything in context of Torah (vv. 18-27). He is able to see in that jarring moment how life with the God of Torah works. In that moment he is able to see that the narcissistic, autonomous agents who go from strength to strength, filled with macho energy and dripping with sexual power, will not prevail—precisely because they are not autonomous. They fall, they are swept way. They vanish like they never were there, like a dream, like a phantom, cannot remember they were even here. How quickly and sadly the Howard Hugheses of the world *evaporate* and the Rosa Parkses of the world *persist* for time to come.

More reflection in vv. 21-22. But now it is not about them; it is about us. I fell for it! I was stubborn, insensitive, hard-hearted, conjuring a world without Torah, stupid, ignorant, brutish.

But now restored to sanity, Torah-focused, back in the commandments:

> Nevertheless, I am continually with you;
> you hold my right hand. (v. 23)

It is not profit but presence that counts, not succeeding, but communion. And then this:

> Whom have I in heaven but you?
> And there is nothing on earth that I desire other than you.
> My flesh and my heart may fail,
> but God is the strength of my heart and my portion forever. (vv. 25-26)

This is a moment of amazing recognition. A recognition of who God is and who I am and who we are. In the end, having nothing but you. In the end, desiring nothing but you: Jesus, Joy of Man's Desiring!

The folks in vv. 1-12 had their desires all confused. There is only one desire. It is God; it is the presence of the Holy One who gives birth and who gives bread.

But notice how far we have come. In v. 1, it is the pay off of obedience. But now obedience has been transposed into blessed community. Obedience is not something coerced, not something imposed, not something extrinsic. It is now an entirely different matter that is relational, given in trust and not in duty.

5. Conclusion to the "until":

> But for me it is good to be near God;
> I have made the Lord God my refuge,
> to tell of all your works. (v. 28)

Not "God is good" (=rewards) as in v. 1. Rather, it is good to be near God. Goodness is now not a product or a commodity or even a gift. It is a presence. The speaker has barely escaped autonomous certitude and ends at peace. He arrived at peace by honest struggle in a moment that could have turned out differently. The psalmist is not shrill or loud, because the issues are too demanding, the costs are too great, and the outcomes are not clear. It all pivots on "until." Who speaks here is a child of Torah, but one who is not protected from dangerous struggle. Finally the poet enters a society of true desire.

V

Our second psalm is 139, and I consider "the religious seduction." It occurs to me that this psalm moves in the opposite direction from Psalm 73. Whereas Psalm 73 concerns one almost talked out of faith, Psalm 139 voices faith that is solid, tight, and deeply assured. Whereas Psalm 73 concerns what I call a *secularist seduction*, Psalm 139 voices what I term a *religious seduction*.

Here speaks faith that is serious, insistent, and buoyant. On the lips of this poet is a God reckoned in the highest Calvinist categories to be omnipotence, omniscience, and omnipresence—all powerful, all knowing, everywhere.

Verses 1-6 assert that God knows all about me, all about us, the one from whom no secret can be hid. And we say "yes."

> You know when I sit down and when I rise up;
> you discern my thoughts from far away.
> You search out my path and my lying down,
> and are acquainted with all my ways. (vv. 2-3)

God knows our thoughts before we speak (v. 4). The thought leads, as does everything for this psalmist, to staggering doxology:

> For such knowledge is too wonderful for me;
> it is so high that I cannot attain it. (v. 6)

It is more than I can understand, more than I can fathom, so unlike anything else that I know.

Verses 7-12 assert that God is everywhere and finally is inescapable. The psalmist probes the extremities of the known world from the top to the bottom, always there is the faithful God, sustaining, protecting, claiming:

> Even there your hand shall lead me,
> and your right hand shall hold me fast. (v. 10)

The psalmist is unlike Amos 9:2-4. The prophet, like Job, wants to escape from God but cannot. But not the psalmist. God is ever present solace. Indeed, the psalmist cites the extreme case, darkness. In that pre-electricity context darkness ominous, dangerous, filled with threats and spirits, like children know, like our failed city streets. But never mind:

> Even the darkness is not dark to you;
> the night is as bright as the day,
> for darkness is as light to you. (v. 12)

And then in vv. 13-18, the psalmist becomes reflective about her own person. I say "her" because these verses bespeak a kind of intimacy, the kind of bodily attentiveness that may or may not be feminine. The language is about the inscrutability of the human person, inward parts, knit in the womb, intricately woven in the depths of the earth, unformed substance. Some think this is a fantasy about egg and semen and formation of the embryo. It is, however, not a lesson in biology. It is a dazzling affirmation about the mystery of life that is hidden in God's powerful will. Like so much about that elemental mystery, faith can reason only so far, and then must break out in doxology:

> How weighty to me are your thoughts, O God!
> How vast is the sum of them!

> I try to count them—they are more than the sand;
> I come to the end—I am still with you. (vv. 17-18)

Indeed, vv. 6, 12, 17-18, at the end of each section, are all doxology, beyond compare, beyond explanation, beyond reason, beyond control—received as elemental truth from which life moves. This person is confident, safe, at home, assured, protected. The conclusion of the poem is a statement of yielding, an invitation to examine, and a certitude about innocence:

> Search me, O God, and know my heart;
> test me and know my thoughts.
> See if there is any wicked way in me,
> and lead me in the way everlasting. (vv. 23-24)

This is Job before the trouble. This is the utterly righteous person known all over the Psalter, committed to an ethic that by any standard is impressive. It is no wonder we cherish this poem of faith.

But, as you may anticipate, my focus is on vv. 19-22. These verses are not only odd. They are an embarrassment, such an embarrassment that we characteristically skip over them, as we skip them in the lectionary for Epiphany 2 (B), Proper 4 (B), Proper 18 (C), and Proper 11 (A). These verses do not make the lectionary anywhere, and it would be better if they were not in the text, in our holy book.

But there they are! They are a prayer that God should kill the wicked who slander me. Who has not known the inclination to pray so? But more than that, the speaker triangles with God against the enemies:

> Do I not hate those who hate you, O Lord?
> And do I not loathe those who rise up against you?
> I hate them with perfect hatred;
> I count them my enemies. (vv. 21-22)

I hate them. I fear them. I despise them. I wish them gone. I do it passionately, completely, fully, totally, without reservation, as an act of virtue. Indeed, I feel as strongly about them negatively as I have felt about God positively for the past eighteen verses. To love God with all your heart and mind and strength easily is to have some commensurate hates. And the ones I hate are the ones who have got it wrong, who hate me, who do evil.

But notice the move. It is not just them and me. It is also God. They do not just hate me. They hate God and they hate the things of God. And they rise up against God. They oppose everything for which God stands—slander, not truth; evil, not good—and are endlessly destructive. This good poet who knows God intimately, who understands the things of God well, who values what God values, nominates herself as surrogate to enact God's hostility because God is not doing it, at least not visibly. God's honor and God's truth are at stake, and someone must take a stand.

Well, you see my line of argument. Absolute certitude in matters of faith and morality is dangerous business. It not only makes for self-assurance. It not only makes for loudness. It makes for brutality. What has happened is that there has come to be an equation—note well: an equation. It could have been a liberal equation or a conservative equation—between my religious moral passion and the things of God, with no slippage between the two. My passions are without question the way God intends the matter.

Do I overread to suggest that such a maneuver amounts to a violation of the first commandment? That command said no compromises, no alternatives, no competitors, no allies. But now it is God and all my religious, moral passions that come along with that love. Perhaps it is a violation of the second commandment as well—no images, no boxing in, no domestications, no chance to force God into a formula or a code or a conclusion, but now God is known by policy statement of the right or of the left. It takes no great imagination, moreover, to think that this psalmist has also violated the third commandment, because God's name is now being used to exhibit my favorite convictions. God made a means and not an end, God's inscrutable holiness that occupies the rest of the psalm, now drawn into my passions. And when God's holiness can be made part of a larger package, it will every time guarantee not love and charity, but hate and brutality and exclusiveness that in the end only mock the God of the commandment.

Thus the concluding statement of innocence in vv. 23-24 is a perfect counterpoint to the passion of vv. 19-22. Anybody who equates his or her own program with the reality of God can be *brutally shrill* toward opponents and *wondrously innocent* about self. I myself know about the passions of vv. 19-22, but they are not justified; for such faith has moved a very long way from yielding obedience to control in the name of God.

VI

So I bid you ponder the *secular temptation* of Psalm 73 with its near decision to give up faith for a better alternative, and the *religious temptation* of Psalm 139 to hold so passionately to faith as to judge all others in the name of God. I thought about these two temptations, and I pondered how to parcel out the psalms. It seemed plausible to me, liberal that I am, that Psalm 73 more likely is a liberal temptation, for some of us mumble about faith claims in order to have it a little better without such scruples, and that seems to leave Psalm 139 for conservatives who tend to be assured and a bit loud.

But then it occurred to me that likely one could reverse the process a bit. Because liberals do tend to be intolerant and impatient with people who are not so enlightened as to get with the program. Then I thought, maybe there is something for conservatives in Psalm 73, because some conservatives do tend to make strident allowances outside the faith for purposes of advantage.

But then I took yet another look at myself, below the level of my self-assigned "liberal" label. And I recognized, in the hidden places I know about, both those temptations of Psalm 73 to accommodate to get along better and of Psalm 139 to whack people who are benighted. I live between these twin temptations, both well, alive, powerful, and seductive. The traffic between them is my liminality, my ambiguity, my place of negotiation, my arena in which God's Spirit may work newness. And then I had the daring thought. I am not the only one this way. Many of you know the *secular temptation to stop loving God* so much because it limits and chastens, and the *religious temptation to love God more* in order to oppose those who are wrong.

And then I thought that your church and my church are in a dangerous, wondrous time when old patterns are gone, new patterns are not clear; we are anxious, on edge, worried, tired—which makes us do crazy things to each other. What would happen if we took these two psalms as a statement about our common liminality, to see in each other—all of us folk—seriously seeking to love God alone with heart and mind and soul, but pulled and unsettled?

The truth is that your church, like mine, is and will be a pluralistic church. Such a church, in my judgment, must give lots of room to sisters and brothers who love God with heart and mind and soul, but who appear to be our enemies. The *certitude of autonomy* and the *certitude of absolutism*, every such certitude, is a danger if we turn our proximate certitudes into addenda to the holiness of God. Your church and mine can continue to vote and scold and claim and crush in loud ways, but none of that in fact serves the first commandment, because such strategies violate the very God whom we intend to love.

VII

So our theme is obedience, the kind of obedience Heschel, Calvin, and Ozick put at the core of our faith. Both the *secularist* in Psalm 73 and the *zealot* in Psalm 139 struggle with obedience. I conclude that in the end obedience is not hard-nosed morality; it is the safety, joy, and well-being of communion that leaves some things a bit open in the community. Thus in Psalm 73:

> Nevertheless I am continually with you;
> you hold my right hand. . . .
> Whom have I in heaven but you?
> And there is nothing on earth that I desire other than you.
> My flesh and my heart may fail,
> but God is the strength of my heart and my portion forever. (vv. 23, 25-26)

And the same in Psalm 139:

> How weighty to me are your thoughts, O God!
> How vast is the sum of them!

I try to count them—they are more than the sand;
I come to the end—I am still with you. (vv. 17-18)

I am continually with you—I am still with you. It is a confession of gratitude and astonishment on which a community can be established that
focuses on a single loyalty (first commandment), that leaves God uncon-
tained (second commandment), and that bootlegs no secondary agenda
(third commandment).

I thought about obedience that is not hard-sell coercive morality. And
that leads me, finally, to reflect on this Jesus. A man concerned for obedience came to him and said:

Good Teacher, what must I do to inherit eternal life? (Mark 10:17)

He answered him, as you know:

Why do you call me good? No one is good but God alone. You know
the commandments: "You shall not murder; You shall not commit
adultery; You shall not steal; You shall not bear false witness; You
shall not defraud; Honor your father and mother." (vv. 18-19)

The commandments are not nuclear science. You know them—do them.
And then Jesus added:

You lack one thing; go, sell what you own, and give the money to
the poor, and you will have treasure in heaven; then come, follow
me. (v. 21)

But he had great possessions. He did first level obedience and perhaps
crowded others to do the same. But second level obedience is of another
sort. Some of us still struggle with first level obedience, being a bit prone to
stealing, killing, committing adultery, coveting. But meeting these requirements is no cause for self-congratulations. For there is immediately another
invitation. And folk like us tend to have great possessions of all sorts.

In the same chapter Jesus continues among his competing disciples. They
are arguing about the control of the future of the church. He interrupts their
intramural competition to think about cups and baptism. And finally this:

It is not so among you; but whoever wishes to become great among
you must be your servant, and whoever wishes to be first among
you must be slave of all. (vv. 43-44)

That in turn led me to two other texts from Jesus. The church must have
been a *community of anxiety* from the outset. Things were never clear,
never settled. And to them he said:

Therefore I tell you, do not worry about your life, what you will eat
or what you will drink, or about your body, what you will wear.
(Matt. 6:25)

And then he said, in yet another place:

> For those who want to save their life will lose it, and those who lose
> their life for my sake, and for the sake of the gospel, will save it. For
> what will it profit them to gain the whole world and forfeit their life?
> Indeed, what can they give in return for their life? (Mark 8:35-37)

The question before the disciples is always the same question, even still
now: What do you want? You want to be right? You want to be in control?
You want to have your way? Or do you want your life? This is a question,
whenever the church is under threat, about keeping and losing, about gain-
ing and forfeiting.

There is something penultimate about all of our certitudes that will not
finally give us what we most want. There is something deeply provisional
about our best causes and our favorite passions, all undermined and desta-
bilized by the God who hems us in, behind and before (Ps. 139:5).

I am aware that what I have said to you may sound like moral relativism.
That, however, is not my theme. My theme, rather, is that the God whom
we are to love without reservation is indeed holy and does not come
prepackaged as certitude. It happens, I believe, that this *failure of certitude*
corresponds to our *canonical context* of pluralism, our *social context* of
dislocation, and our *intimate condition* of liminality. The one we are to
love, cherish, and obey is inscrutable and cannot be reduced to pet projects,
even Calvinist pet projects.

Imagine what would happen if we in our churches understood and
embraced the faith of the psalmist:

> Whom have I in heaven but you?
> And there is nothing on earth that I desire other than you.
> My flesh and my heart may fail,
> But God is the strength of my heart and my portion forever. (Ps. 73:25-26)

We should be freed for the God to whom darkness and light are just alike.
I heard a prayer recently that had this phrasing in it:

> Forgive our exaggerated responses to life's uncertainties. Assure us of
> your care so that we might release our anxious grasp on all inadequate
> means of salvation and reach again for your beloved child. Amen.

This is a deep and urgent moment in the life of the church, dear sisters and
brothers, when we may move out from under our mutual coercions to new
life with God. But it takes some relinquishing of what we treasure. If we do
not relinquish for the sake of God's holiness, we shall grow to be a scandal
in the world. Or as that great cynical Calvinist theologian, Mark Twain, put
it in a way that may pertain to our shared intransigence:

> He is a good person . . . in the worst sense of the word.

Neighborliness and the Limits of Power in God's Realm: On the Second Great Commandment

W‌HEN OUR MOTHERS AND FATHERS ARRIVED AT SINAI THEY HAD JUST come from the land of Pharaoh. They remembered that land well, and all our mothers and fathers have remembered that land well since that time. It had been a place of great corporate wealth in which the powerful controlled all the public processes, in which the little ones were used up and discarded, in which the weak ones were abused and oppressed, in which the marginal ones were silenced and coerced. They had groaned and cried out, until they had finally attracted the attention of Yahweh. And then they were liberated! They remembered it well; they told their children about it endlessly. But they could never explain their departure. They regarded it as a miracle about which they could only break out in song and dance.

I

And then they arrived at Sinai. The mountain was severe and forbidding, and dangerous. The God who sojourns there gave them a thesis sentence:

> Now therefore, if you obey my voice and keep my covenant, you shall be my treasured possession out of all the peoples. Indeed, the whole earth is mine, but you shall be for me a priestly kingdom and a holy nation. (Exod. 19:5-6)

From the outset they understood their oddity. They were a peculiar people, rescued inexplicably and now recruited into an alternative service. They gladly exchanged the unbearable, exploitative rule of Pharaoh for the governance of Yahweh. They did that even before they knew the specifics. But they reasoned, better to be with a God who liberates than a power that oppresses. This is the God who had said, almost like a mantra, "Let my people go." And so they promised, in anticipation:

> Everything that the Lord has spoken we will do. (v. 8)

They signed on without reading any of the fine print.

But then the meeting got down to specifics. The ominous voice from the mountain, as we have seen, had spoken three times to secure God's own holiness from excessive human certitude:

- no other gods
- no graven images
- no wrongful use of the name.

But the voice continued, moving from divine holiness to human community. You know the agenda:

- Sabbath
- honor
- no killing
- no adultery
- no stealing
- no crooked courts
- no acquisitive coveting.

The voice was terse and abrupt, without justification or explanation, or even punishment. Just NO! Cynthia Ozick again:

> Another way of reflecting on the why is to note that the Jews vis-à-vis nihilism, stand for No; not the No of nihilism, but the No against nihilism, the No that presses for restraint. . . . They begin with lo, the Hebrew word for No: no tignov, do not steal. Punkt. The Torah the Jews carry stands for No, for all the things we ordinary mortals want to do and take glee in doing.[1]

Think of it: a mountain utterance as a line of defense against nihilism! Think of nihil—nothingness. It is not a philosophical idea. It is a power visible in the human community wherever the big ones eat the little ones. Pharaoh is a force for the nihil. The Israelites know all about it. And Sinai is an alternative to nihil. The nihil showed itself powerfully on Friday, but it did not prevail. The nihil shows again in the holocaust. The nihil shows again wherever enormous wealth devours poor ones, where blacks and whites, male and female, Protestant and Catholic, Christian and Muslim go for the throat. Sinai intends otherwise. Sinai insists otherwise. The otherwise is premised on Yahweh's holiness, but it comes concretely to concern *others* in the human community.

Later Moses explicated all this in the book of Deuteronomy. The book of Deuteronomy is Israel's "neighbor-book," a most revolutionary social vision. This same Moses from Sinai, remembering the first three Commandments, said lyrically:

> For the Lord your God is God of gods and Lord of lords, the great God, mighty and awesome . . . (Deut. 10:17a)

But before Moses is finished, characteristically, he moves to the neighborhood:

> . . . who is not partial and takes no bribe, who executes justice for the orphan and the widow, and who loves the strangers, providing them food and clothing. (vv. 17b-18)

And then the mandate:

> You shall also love the stranger, for you were strangers in the land
> of Egypt. (v. 19)

The great God above who commands gods and angels and principalities
is preoccupied with *orphans, widows,* and *strangers.* Deuteronomy at the
center of the old Torah is a socio-economic-political vision for the little ones:

  • orphans because they have no daddy in a patriarchal society;
  • widows because they have no husbands in a patriarchal society.
No daddy or husband, no bread-winner, no advocate, no protection, no
redeemer, endlessly exposed to the devouring power of the big and ruthless
ones. I do not need to mention the stranger, the undocumented worker, the
ones who cannot ever pretend to belong, whose life consists of occasional
labor, seasonal work, and endless anxiety about visas.

This basic resolve of Yahweh echoes throughout the scroll:

> Bring out the full tithe of your produce for that year; . . . the Levites,
> because they have no allotment or inheritance with you, as well as
> the resident aliens, the orphans, and the widows in your towns, may
> come and eat their fill so that the Lord your God may bless you in
> all the work that you undertake. (Deut. 14:28-29)
> Rejoice, . . . you and your sons and your daughters, your male and
> female slaves, as well as the Levites, the strangers, the orphans, and
> the widows resident in your towns. (Deut. 16:14; see v. 11)
> You shall not deprive a resident alien or an orphan of justice; you
> shall not take a widow's garment in pledge. . . . When you reap your
> harvest in your field and forget a sheaf in the field, you shall not go
> back to get it; it shall be left for the alien, the orphan, and the
> widow, so that the Lord your God may bless you in all your under-
> takings. When you beat your olive trees, do not strip what is left; it
> shall be for the alien, the orphan, and the widow. . . . When you
> gather the grapes of your vineyard, do not glean what is left; it shall
> be for the alien, the orphan, and the widow. Remember that you
> were a slave in the land of Egypt; therefore I am commanding you
> to do this. (Deut. 24:17, 19-22; see 26:12-13)

The teaching concerns *material resources* and *worship activity*; Moses
knew no separation or dualism.

II

The same issue of a neighbor surfaces in a challenge to Jesus. Coming again
to Jesus, you remember the question they ask (Mark 12:28-34). It was not
a trick question, but an endless rabbinic question, always asked, always
answered, rather like endless Stanley Cup playoffs. They asked him, as they

asked each other, "Which Commandment is first of all?" And you know his answer. Surely they thought he had answered rightly.

Except he did not even pause. He went right on into v. 31 without missing a beat:

> The second is this, "You shall love your neighbor as yourself."
> There is no other commandment greater than these. (Mark 12:31)

It is second, it comes with the first. Perhaps some said, "We only asked for one, not two." But he says, no Commandment is greater than these two. Jesus had well studied Deuteronomy and surely knew about the God of gods who attends to the vulnerable. He knew, moreover, the Commandments from Sinai; he knew that you got the neighbor commands in the same moment with the same authority. Moses had linked them and Jesus keeps them connected. You cannot in this tradition say "God" without saying "neighbor," nearly hyphenated, "God-neighbor." Until we arrive at the cadences of the epistle:

> Those who say, "I love God," and hate their brothers or sisters, are liars; for those who do not love a brother or sister whom they have seen, cannot love God whom they have not seen. The commandment we have from him is this: those who love God must love their brothers and sisters also. (1 John 4:20-21)

It is ironic that when Jesus is asked this question, he goes first to the shema of Deut. 6:4-5 as any good Jew would have done. But then much less obviously, he pulls the second Commandment from a place we would have thought obscure. The neighbor command is situated in Lev. 19:18, a chapter, as you know, just between chapters 18 and 20 on all sorts of sexual issues. He pulled this one out and made it prominent, even inescapable for us. And when he said this, his questioners agreed. He said to them:

> You are not far from the kingdom. (Mark 12:34)

It is kingdom newness to see *the mandate of God-neighbor*. And since that time, our community has been endlessly haunted by the wonderment: Who is my neighbor? And generally we understand this better than we want, because the neighbor question is in fact not that difficult.

III

So my theme is neighbor. We know very well about love of neighbor, and the missional mandates and the justice issues that arise from it. I refocus only slightly to have you consider the church as a neighborhood, members as neighbors, who are to be loved as we love ourselves. I make this obvious point, because our common life is nearly destroyed by forgetting the simple, elemental mandate of neighborliness that is intrinsic in the God command.

But there is more than that, and I want to pause with you over three passages and then some obvious conclusions. It is thought by many scholars
that Deut. 15:1-18 is the core teaching of the Moses tradition, the most radical Torah requirement in the practice of neighborliness.[2] It is there the *year
of release*. It was conventional in that ancient world that if one owed a debt,
it was worked off as a day laborer, the greater the debt, the more days
worked off. This teaching, however, provides that if a debt is held "against
a neighbor" (v. 2), the tenure of such work is limited to six years, no matter how great the debt. At the end of six years, the debt is cancelled, and the
debtor is free to go home unencumbered. This was an extraordinary
requirement to assure that there should be no permanent underclass in the
neighborhood, no enduringly disadvantaged people. It was a most radical
upsetting of conventional economic patterns in order to bind creditors and
debtors to each other in a neighborly way, to curb the power of creditors in
order to limit the hurt or indignity to debtors. That is, it is an effort to bring
power relations into a *covenantal fabric of neighborliness.*

There are three things I want you to notice about this biblical mandate
on the lips of Moses.

The first is the odd juxtaposition of vv. 4 and 11. Verse 11 is better
known to us because Jesus quoted it in Mark 14:7, "You always have the
poor with you." The verse in context means you have to keep doing this
release always, keep breaking vicious cycles of indebtedness and power in
order to have a neighborhood. In v. 4 Moses says, "The poor will cease out
of the land" (my translation); that sounds like a contradiction of v. 11. But
v. 4 means this action will really work. It will make a difference. Thus vv. 4
and 11 together assert: It matters if you do it; keep doing it always.

The year of release is perhaps the oddest, most distinctive, most demanding requirement for loving neighbor. It sets the community of ancient Israel
apart from all other communities in insisting that power must be limited
and handled differently if there is to be a neighborhood. This may strike
you as simple *common sense*, but it is a special common sense discernable
only among those already committed to the full *love of God* who is the God
of all the neighbors.

Patrick Miller has observed that this "year of release" is a special case of
what he calls a more general *sabbatic principle* that pervades biblical
ethics.[3] More specifically it shows up as Sabbath, as work stoppage in
which everyone in the neighborhood is permitted rest and free time, all the
way from lords and ladies to servants and donkeys and oxen, everyone in
the neighborhood in order to break the vicious cycles of consumption and
production. Writ most largely, the sabbatic principle shows up as *jubilee
year*, that fiftieth year in which all members of the community receive back
what is theirs, what is needed for full membership in the community. Biblical ethics is preoccupied with the major insistence that power in the community must be deployed differently in order to have a neighborhood. It

must be deployed this way and not in the ways of the world, because God wills it. And where power in the community is deployed sabbatically, there the God known in Jesus Christ rules, or we may say, there comes the Kingdom of God. Thus the first thing to notice is the insistence in vv. 4 and 11.

The second thing to notice, which can hardly be seen in English translation, concerns Hebrew grammar. But all those who have successfully completed Hebrew grammar will remember the absolute infinitive. This is an odd habit of grammar whereby the verb is repeated for emphasis, so that if you want to say, "really give," you say in Hebrew, "give, give." What interests us is that in this one Commandment of Moses, there are five absolute infinitives, more than in any other command. Moses speaks with great intensity, and means the practice to be done as the life-or-death mark of covenantal fidelity. So in this passage, we have:

- bless, bless (v. 4)
- hear, hear (v. 5)
- open, open, (v. 8)
- lend, lend (v. 8)
- give, give (v. 10)

I mean *really!*

The third element to be noticed is that in vv. 8-10, Moses requires that the poor debtor, when sent back into the economy, shall not go out "empty-handed" (mark that word), but "you shall not be tight fisted, but you shall give liberally and without defrauding," so that the poor neighbor may have economic viability. This is something like overcompensation or reparations, in which the rich and powerful must do extra for the weak and poor, because it is the will of the God whom we love, because it is the *sine qua non* of covenantal community.

This demand in this odd community that loves God is a delight, but a delight only to those who love God. For any other, it is an unreasonable demand and hardship. But Moses concludes:

> Do not consider it a hardship. (v. 18)
> Remember that you were a slave in the land of Egypt, and the LORD
> your God redeemed you. (v. 15)

That you are redeemed permits and requires a deeply different deployment of power in the community.

Now you may rightly wonder why I have spent time on this strange text. The text clearly is concerned with economics, and our issues here are mostly ecclesial. So perhaps it is a stretch. I will tell you my thinking on the pertinence of this text. Two linkages. First, as Patrick Miller has shown, all "forgiveness" in the Bible—including in the New Testament—is about economics in the first instant.[4] The primal forgiveness is of *debts,* and all other forgivenesses are extrapolations. The year of release is about forgiveness as a basic condition for a neighborhood. Second, the real internal issues before the church, the ones that see us clawing each others' eyes out, concern power. This text is about an evangelical adjudication of power between the strong and the weak, between the haves and have-nots.

So I thought, with the intensity of Moses with five infinitive absolutes and with the scholarly judgment that this is the core practice for loving neighbors, that this text has a deep relevance to our issues, because it invites a radical rethinking about a neighborly church in obedience to the gospel, whereby strong and weak, rich and poor, haves and have nots live together differently because of gospel obedience.

As the powerful and wealthy are here enjoined by Moses not to be tight-fisted or grudging or hard-hearted, but to give liberally, Moses says:

> You should rather open your hand, willingly lending enough to meet the need, whatever it may be. Be careful that you do not entertain a mean thought, thinking, "The seventh year, the year of remission, is near," and therefore view your needy neighbor with hostility and give nothing; your neighbor might cry to the Lord against you, and you would incur guilt. Give liberally and be ungrudging when you do so, for on this account the Lord your God will bless you in all your work and in all that you undertake.
> (vv. 8-10)

Now I know it is money, that deepest symbol of power and control, that is to be handed over to the undeserving in a way that is contrary to all worldly practice. Think of it. And think about the transactions in the church that are not primarily about *financial capital*. They are rather about other kinds of capital that are to be handed over to the undeserving, in a way contrary to all worldly practice.

The first of these is *political capital*, the power to dominate and control the decision-making processes of church courts, majority rule, both by community majorities and by manipulative wording, etc., etc. If we transpose this most radical requirement for love of neighbor, it suggests to me *ceding over power* to those who are indebted, needy, undeserving, not to seek control over them, but yielding in generosity to them.

The second mode of capital into which I would transpose this teaching of Moses concerns *moral capital*, the capacity to occupy, by passion and by study and by rhetoric and by fidelity, the morally high ground on an issue and the leverage to make it stick. A surface impression would lead me to think that conservatives easily seem to occupy high moral ground on sexuality issues and to work from their moral capital. In like manner, a surface impression leads me to think that liberals are easily seen to occupy high moral ground on economic issues and to work from that moral capital. It is easy, in either case or in both cases, to imagine one's opponents on lower moral ground, to think they take such stands because of hard-heartedness or stupidity or lack of faith.

But if we extrapolate from the text that urges the yielding of moral capital for the sake of the neighbor, we remember that the inclusion of the neighbor in the neighborhood is more crucial than the control of moral capital or political capital. The radicality can be seen if we imagine that neighborliness is more important than good economics or good politics or good morality or good orthodoxy.

Now I am aware that such an argument is against all of our ordered inclinations. Surely some would think if you compromise *political capital*, the church will be in confusion, and if you compromise *moral capital*, things will fall apart. No doubt some said to Moses, "The year of release will destroy the fabric of the economy." And I can imagine Moses—with Sinai ringing in his ears—answering, "Neighbor, neighbor, neighbor."

You see, sisters and brothers, the second Great Commandment is inordinately demanding and radical. It is premised on the will of God who offers and enacts a radical covenantal otherness that entails risk, self-giving, even yielding for the sake of the other. The problem with too much of the church is that we shadow and imitate the world. But this ethic of neighbor is about covenant, about baptism, about being crucified to new life. So the neighbor may not be empty-handed, financially, politically, morally.

IV

My second text is more familiar. It is familiar to me since it was answer to question Number 72 in my catechism of nurture:

> In which passage of Holy Scripture do we find the humiliation and exaltation of Christ briefly expressed? We find the humiliation and exaltation of Christ briefly expressed in the passage Phil. 2:5-11:
> "Have this mind among yourselves, which is yours in Christ Jesus, who, though he was in the form of God, did not count equality with God a thing to be grasped, but emptied himself, taking the form of a servant, being born in the likeness of men. And being found in human form, he humbled himself and became obedient unto death, even death on a cross. Therefore God has highly exalted him and bestowed on him the name which is above every name, that at the name of Jesus every knee should bow, in heaven and on earth and under the earth, and every tongue confess that Jesus Christ is Lord, to the glory of God the Father." [RSV]

We had to memorize it. We had to memorize it for Saturday confirmation before Friday night, or no basketball game.

As you know, this lyrical text is taken by many of us to be the quintessential articulation of the gospel. As you know, the phrase "emptied himself" is a theological tag word. Jesus emptied himself of power, power rightly his, to be available and vulnerable and at risk as a human person.

The Greek word for "empty," *kenosis*, is fundamental to our faith, speaking our confession against all gnosticism and against all New Age alternatives, and some think against the Jesus Seminar. We take it that in Jesus of Nazareth the capacity to save and redeem and make all things new is given in his embrace of such extreme vulnerability.

The lyric affirms that it is this obedience to death that is foundational for the exaltation of Jesus, as we say in the creed, "to the right hand of the Father." Thus the humiliation and exaltation, as my catechism put it, is supremely about the Friday of wretchedness and the Sunday of exuberance that became the pivot of our confession of faith. It is clear in this doxology that the *Friday of emptiness* is the first step and precondition for the *Sunday of fullness*. The sequence and the juxtaposition are crucial. We all know that and gladly affirm it.

From this glad confession, I make two linkages. First, I had thought of this text in any case after Deut. 15 as the one in the New Testament that seemed pertinent to the second Great Commandment. But then I noticed a more compelling linkage between the two texts. The *kenosis* in Phil. 2:7 is well known. As I looked at Deut. 15, I read in vv. 13-14:

> When you send a male slave out from you a free person, you shall
> not send him out empty-handed. Provide liberally out of your flock,
> your threshing floor, and your wine press, thus giving to him some
> of the bounty with which the Lord your God has blessed you.

"Do not send him out empty-handed." Would you believe that the Greek version of the Old Testament in Deut. 15:13 is *kenon*, "not *empty*"? The text points to Phil. 2:7:

- Do not send him out empty;
- He emptied himself.

Same word! The neighbor is not to be empty. You are to *fill* the hand of the empty neighbor by your generosity. Indeed, Jesus is the full neighbor who *empties himself* in order to fill the neighbor. The odd evangelical anticipation in Deut. 15 and embodiment in Jesus of Nazareth is the transfer of power, the yielding of power, the ceding over of power, for the sake of the neighbor, for the sake of the world. Deut. 15 and Phil. 2 share the summons to *fill by emptying*, propelled by the love of God.

The second connection I make is this. Phil. 2:6-11 concerns the mystery of Christ, in the church's lyrical way of saying "truly divine, truly human." It is, however, easily recognized that Paul finally is not preoccupied here with a christological statement, as wondrous as it is. He is here, as he usually is, a pastor helping a local congregation come to terms with the concrete reality of its life: disputes about leadership, arguments about morality, interpretations about polity, quarrels about sacraments, all the usual stuff of church disagreement. It is an ecclesial issue that prompts Paul when he makes an argument that the church, baptized as we are, is not to conduct its business or settle its disputes like any other community. We are bound to a God for whom the neighbor comes first.

And so Paul names the categories of life in the church: *encouragement* in Christ, *consolation* from love, *sharing* in the spirit, *compassion, sympathy.* Those five ingredients are fundamental markings of the community:

- encouragement in Christ—the one who empowers folk at their extremity
- consolation from love—comfort outside leverage
- sharing in the spirit, for it is the spirit who makes generosity possible;
- compassion—being together in suffering
- sympathy—the ability to be attentive to the other in need and in pain.

These are premises. They are introduced by an "if." Paul assumes in the "if" that these premises are granted and operational. We are all agreed in these.

On that basis, he issues his pastoral imperatives:

- *Same mind*—mind of Christ
- *same love*—self-giving, yielding, deferential
- *full accord*
- *one mind.*

How could it be, liberals and conservatives, a quarrel as old as our community is old, when all is given over to the Christ who walks in none of our savage ideologies?

Now he comes to cases, not romantic faith talk, but about the imperatives of an evangelical polity:

- Do nothing from selfish ambition
- Do nothing from conceit
- In humility, regard others as better than yourselves.

You want that line again?

In humility, regard others as better than yourselves.

These words need no comment or interpretation, but only the chance for pondering. As you know, I am not making this up. It is there in the text; talk about inerrant and infallible. There it is: Regard others as better than yourselves—better in faith, better in discernment, better in stewardship, better in leadership, better in morality, better in orthodoxy, better in social analysis. Paul keeps piling it on: Look not to your own interests, but to the interests of others.

The problem of course is that our interests feel so much like the interests of God. So in Psalm 139, as we have seen, the psalmist assumes his hates are God's hates. But Paul is clear. The seduction is our own interests, because nobody is disinterested. The Christian community is a community that holds to the odd conviction that the neighbor—the one so odd, so stupid, so recalcitrant, so misguided, so careless, so rigid—is superior.

Not easy for us Calvinists who are knowledgeable, bright, thoughtful, passionate, convinced! Paul's antidote to our resistance is the mind of Christ, the giving, yielding, generous, emptying mind of Christ. Paul's utilization of the Christ hymn invites that local congregation to go underneath morality and behind orthodoxy, to the mood and person and presence of Christ where our most tendentious disputes are reduced to second-rate importance.

Paul understood the awkwardness of this little congregation in the ocean of the Roman empire. He wanted the baptized community to enact its odd faith in concrete, visible ways in response to the second Great Commandment based on the first. He believed, because of the Friday-Easter mystery, that the church could conduct its life differently.

I speak to you about this little baptized community in an ocean of secular greed and brutality in our own time; our Lord is scandalized when the church forgets its underpinning and imagines that the power and the truth of the gospel can be contained in our moral, dogmatic leverage of each other.

The early church was an *emergency community*, in Paul's horizon, as the Sinai community was an *emergency community* in the ancient world. Neither circumcised Israel nor baptized church could afford simply to extrapolate from the world around, but had to make a leap of trust and risk for life together. Do you think I overstate, brothers and sisters, if I say to you that at the end of the twentieth century, our church is an *emergency community* in which the interests of the Crucified One call us beyond our conventionality to the risk of the Friday-Sunday God who makes all things new?

Paul is here like a nervous mother, wondering how the kids will do, summoning them to their best but worried about neglectful forgetting. And so he says, "Complete my joy." Make me happy. Be who you are. Get out of your quarrelsome slots into the mind of Christ who characteristically pushes the envelope of the first Great Commandment straight into the second. Let the world see that the truth of Friday-Sunday concerns a different human community.

V

From Philippians 2, I move to my third and final text, again the pastor Paul, who in 2 Cor. 8:1-15 has become a regional stewardship director. Paul is trying to raise the annual budget for the bereft Jerusalem church. Like every good fundraiser, he appeals to recent success stories.

Take for example, he says, the churches of Macedonia. In a severe ordeal of affliction that he does not name,

> Their abundant joy and their extreme poverty have overflowed in a
> wealth of generosity on their part. (v. 2)

I always think, when I read Paul—not understanding Greek syntax that much—that he must pile up phrases as we sometimes do in pastoral prayers. Perhaps the phrases should not be scrutinized too closely. Except they are astonishing: They had *joy and poverty*. And they enacted "a wealth of generosity." He tells of them "begging for the privilege of sharing" (v. 4), because they first gave themselves to the Lord. They embraced the first Great Commandment, thereby being completely free for the second, neighborly Commandment. Their poverty, gladly yielded, turned into abundance. This is the "new math" rooted in the generosity of God. It is this same math that left the residue, after 5,000 ate, of twelve baskets of bread, and after a meal for 4,000, a remnant of seven baskets. This is the new math rooted in the abundance of God whom we name as creator of heaven and earth, who wills abundance and fruitfulness. One summary of the doctrine of creation is "there is more," because God's creation is the gift that keeps on giving.

You see, the evangelical faith of the Macedonians, who were baptized, did not accept zero-sum ideology based on the myth of scarcity. The myth of scarcity that drives the Western economy and much of the Western church is rooted in the denial of God's abundance. There is not enough to go around. There will not be enough to go around. Keep what you have. Get more. Protect, seize, guard. It is an act of atheism that is very deep in the practice of much greed, fear, and anxiety. And those of us who are children of the Depression believe it most and know it best.

But it is unfaith. The alternative, the alternative rooted in God's abundance and enacted in the second Commandment, is that giving generates more, because beyond all of our generosity is the bottomless generosity of God. They gave themselves to the generosity of God, and then there was ample ground for giving. The claim of abundance over scarcity is not simply a nice theological idea, but it is a concrete communal practice. Generosity transforms.

And the ground for such a claim? It is the same ground to which Paul always appeals. It is Jesus:

> For you know the generous act of our Lord Jesus Christ, that though he was rich, yet for your sakes he became poor, so that by his poverty you might become rich. (v. 9)

Jesus was rich, rich toward God, rich from God—as we say at Columbia Theological Seminary, with a big endowment, well-endowed. He became poor. That is, he emptied himself. He gave himself away. He held nothing back. He enacted the second Commandment, taking his neighbor as better than himself. It was not a rash act. It was "for your sakes," for the sake of the neighborhood. The gospel is not premised on supply-side theories. Exactly the opposite! That is the concrete, worldly scandal of the gospel, a willingly embraced poverty making many rich: many widows and orphans, many publicans and sinners and lepers, many marginal, disqualified people, many people unlike us, hovering on the outside, yearning for the inside. He did this. He has broken the deep cycle of scarcity with an overwhelming flood of generosity.

So I speak to you about zero-sum and supply-side and trickle-down—and generosity. Sisters and brothers. There is enough. There is enough power, enough orthodoxy, enough morality, enough, more than enough, a good measure, pressed down, shaken together, running over (Luke 6:38). This is the one who

> is able to accomplish abundantly far more than all we can ask or imagine. (Eph. 3:20)

Jews have a liturgical word for it: *dayenu!* IT IS ENOUGH!

So imagine, the imitators of Christ who power the church are not those who are starchy about sexual orthodoxy, not those who are as stiff about economics. Those who power the church are those who give themselves up in generosity, who trust in the wealth of the creator and who ponder the self-giving of Christ that they become poor—in power, in morality, in piety—in order to make many others rich. I find this mind-boggling, and I hope you do as well. Think about the energy and the magnetism that are given if and when the church is seen as a community so in love with brothers and sisters that all coerciveness and bitterness and domination evaporate. Or is it not possible? Was the emptying of Friday in vain? Was the exuberance of Sunday only a rumor?

Paul is sober at the end of his appeal. He understands we are in the real world:

> I do not mean that there should be relief for others and pressure on you, but it is a question of a fair balance between your present abundance and their need, so that their abundance may be for your need, in order that there may be a fair balance. (2 Cor. 8:13-14)

But then, after "fair balance," Paul must quote from the manna story of Exodus 16, all about abundance that legitimates generosity, and generosity that evokes abundance:

> The one who had much did not have too much, and the one who had little did not have too little. (v. 15)

Dayenu!

It is odd in Deuteronomy 15, Philippians 2, and 2 Corinthians 8, that every text comes down to economics—year of release, the interest of others, poverty and wealth. It is the way of the Bible to stay very close to lived reality, but to resituate our most anxious agenda in the context of the truthfulness of God. It may be that at bottom our problem is a kind of atheism that does not trust God's generosity. Without generosity of mind and heart, the second Commandment is null and void.

VI

Four conclusions of a rather random character:

1. I commend to you a book by Raimon Panikkar, that great Indian thinker, titled *Cultural Disarmament*. He is thinking large about the domination of the West, but his way of putting the matter is germane to the crisis in the church. He writes:

> Peace is not possible without disarmament. But the required disarmament is not only nuclear, military, or economic. There is also a need for a cultural disarmament, a disarmament of the dominant culture, which threatens to become a monoculture capable of engulfing all other cultures and finally along with them. . . . It is an all but immediate evidence that military disarmament is impossible without cultural disarmament.[5]

Brothers and sisters, I have been speaking to you about disarmament. Disarmament means to honor those who are neighbors unlike us, who are baptized, for the church on many issues is now pluralistic in ways it has never needed to be in our memory. It occurs to me that the cross is the ultimate disarmament, "did not take equality with God a thing to be grasped, but emptied himself." Baptism is our decision to live and risk in the name of the Crucified who is utterly disarmed.

2. I ran across a speech given by Judge Learned Hand on May 21, 1944, that is, two weeks before D-Day. Learned Hand was an important but not well known judge in New York City. He was invited to speak at the great annual festival in Central Park for the swearing in of 150,000 naturalized citizens. It was a great day of exuberant public celebration. In his stunning address, later likened to the Gettysburg Address in its eloquent, simple power, Hand told the new citizens:

> The spirit of liberty is the spirit which is not too sure it is right; the spirit of liberty is the spirit which seeks to understand the merits of other men and women; the spirit of liberty is the spirit which weights their interests alongside its own without bias; the spirit of liberty remembers that not even a sparrow falls to earth unheeded. The spirit of liberty is the spirit of Him who, nearly two thousand years ago, taught man that lesson it has never learned, but has never quite forgotten, that there may be a kingdom where the least shall be heard and considered side by side with the greatest.[6]

I was deeply moved when I read this about five months ago. I had this present address on my mind, and I noticed this connection: Look to the interests of others and not your own.

But of course I also noticed that this great judge, in a civic address, refers to Jesus, sparrows, and a new kingdom. We are the ones who know about these matters. It is fair to cite this civic address, I judge, because we Calvinists are the most civic of all believers, and because we Calvinists have a deep inclination to be too sure we are right. The kingdom where the least shall be heard has as a prerequisite not being so sure, not so sure and therefore given liberty, "the glorious freedom of the children of God," "for where the Spirit of the LORD is, there is freedom" (Rom. 8:21 [NAB]; 2 Cor. 3:17).

3. I have said these things to you, sisters and brothers, in the name of the Father and the Son and the Spirit, that we may together remember our baptism, renounce the Devil and all his works. We will name these works of the Devil differently. But we are all baptized into a new neighborliness that is genuine and open-ended, with a God-given freedom to move beyond our interests, our fears, our hurts, and our hopes, to the interest of the neighbor.

It is clear in all of the texts I have cited—Deuteronomy 15, Philippians 2, 2 Corinthians 8—that the community is rooted in *odd generosities*, summoned to *odd obediences*, destined for *odd well-being and joy*. Our sort of church has become casual, so it seems to me, in doing our business the way the world does its business. And now, in what I take to be an emergency, we are invited in our baptism to have among us the same mind that we have in Jesus Christ.

4. I finish by a second reference to that great cynical Calvinist theologian, Mark Twain. He was asked, "Do you believe in infant baptism?" He answered: "Believe in it, Hell, I have seen it." Our task now is to let it be seen.

7   Truth-Telling as Subversive Obedience

THE NINTH COMMANDMENT—"YOU SHALL NOT BEAR FALSE WITNESS against your neighbor"—has not been an accent point in biblical ethics or an emphasis in Mosaic-covenantal faith. Moreover the commandment is easily reduced to a kind of banal moralism, as though "lying" is a bad thing and should be avoided, a notion which is as thin as one can make the commandment. We here reconsider this commandment both as an exploration in interpretive method, and to see how this commandment may be a primal carrier of a Mosaic-covenantal vision of reality that is oddly pertinent to our moment of social crisis.[1]

1

It is important at the outset to recognize that the commandment, expressed in absolute terms, is part of the decalogue given at "the holy mountain." As such it constitutes a part of the most elemental insistence of the Sinai covenant.[2] More than that, it voices an important dimension of the Mosaic vision of social reality and social possibility.

The commandment brings into stark juxtaposition two terms that assure its covenantal intent: "neighbor—false." The prohibition is not simply against "false witnesses," but it is a false witness against *your neighbor*, that is, a fellow-member of the covenant community. The horizon of the prohibition is the well-being of the neighbor and the enhancement of the neighborhood. More broadly the prohibition concerns practices and conditions that make a neighborhood viable and genuinely human.

The antithetical term here is "false" (*šeqer*). In the second version of the decalogue, the term is *šû'*, but the intention is not different (Deut. 5:20). The term "false" concerns utterance that distorts or misrepresents or skews. Viable community, according to Mosaic vision, depends upon accurate, reliable utterance. The process of community is profoundly vulnerable to distorted speech which inevitably skews social relations and social structures.

The commandment, however, is even more particular. It alludes to the precise setting in which false utterance is possible, seductive, and dangerous. "You shall not answer with false testimony." The verb "answer" and the noun "witness" indicate that we are concerned with solemn utterance under oath in a judicial context. In short, the commandment seeks to assure a reliable, independent judiciary. The Ten Commandments, as a whole, seek to bring every facet of social life under the aegis of Yahweh and into the context of covenant. This ninth commandment concerns the court system, and insists that evidence given in court must be honest and reliable and uncontaminated by interest. It is astonishing that in its most elemental summary, Yahwistic ethics insists upon a reliable, independent judiciary as one of the pillars of viable human life.[3]

It is clear that the notion of a court that gives reliable utterance is a continuing concern of the tradition of Moses. In Exod. 18:13-23, offered as a Mosaic innovation, Moses is instructed to find reliable judicial officers:

> You should also look for able men among all the people, men who fear God, are trustworthy, and hate dishonest gain. (v. 21)[4]

And in speaking of judges subsequently,

> You must not distort justice; you must not show partiality; and you must not accept bribes, for a bribe blinds the eyes of the wise and subverts the cause of those who are in the right. Justice, and only justice, you shall pursue. (Deut. 16:19-20)

The courts are seen to be crucial because, in social disputes that relate to political, economic matters, it is the capacity and responsibility of the court to *determine, limit, and shape reality*. And therefore if power and interest can intrude upon truth—by way of influence, manipulation, or bribe—then truth has no chance. It is reduced to power, and the powerless are then easily and predictably exploited.

Recent public events make altogether evident that a reliable, independent judiciary is indispensable to a viable society. In the U.S., it was the courts that were finally able to insist upon a constitutional vision of human and civil rights when all other aspects of the public process had failed. In old colonial powers and in the dictatorships of "banana republics," it is often only the judiciary that prevents legitimated exploitation and brutality. Indeed, even as I write this, it is a "truth commission" with something like quasi-judicial powers at work in South Africa that has a chance to put to rest the long nightmare of brutality in that society. This commandment insists, in a direct and unadorned way, that "social truth" inheres in neighborly transactions and is not open to the easy impact of raw power that denies human reality. The commandment guarantees that *reality* is not an innocent product of *power*. The future of humanity is not open to endless "reconstruction" by those who have the capacity to do so, but must adhere to what is "on the ground."

II

The commandment is likely articulated in a simple, face-to-face agrarian society. It is a simple requirement that neighbors not distort shared social reality. But as is characteristic in biblical traditions, this simple agrarian provision is transformed into a larger social concern by the imaginative power of the prophets. The requirement of truth-telling is matured by the prophets, first by enlarging its scope to include royal reality with its penchant for distorted public policy, and second by turning a "rule of evidence" into a Yahwistic claim. Examples of this larger maneuver include Nathan's word to David concerning the violation of Uriah (2 Sam. 12:7-12) and Elijah's word against Jezebel, who had manipulated truth by royal power (1 Kings 21:19-24). In both cases, it is important that it is the issue of truth that is at stake in the prophetic confrontation. Both David and Jezebel have born false witness, David against Uriah, Jezebel against Naboth. Such distorting actions cannot stand, even if performed by the royal house.

In the prophetic period, powerful royal interests were so skillful at the management of symbols and the control of information ("disformation") that scenarios of "virtual" reality could be constructed completely remote from lived reality. The tradition of Jeremiah is preoccupied with *falseness* whereby managed reality yields a phony sense of life and well-being.[5] The poet counters such control:

> From the least to the greatest of them,
> everyone is greedy for unjust gain;
> and from prophet to priest,
> everyone deals falsely.
> They have treated the wound of my people carelessly,
> saying "Peace, peace,"
> when there is no peace. (Jer. 6:13-14; cf. 8:11)

Now the concern is not one citizen deceiving another, as it might have been in a neighborly, agrarian society. Now it is the great organs of news and information in society being managed to serve distorted public ends, calculated to deceive on a grand scale.

Working the same rhetoric, the prophet Ezekiel holds religious leadership peculiarly guilty for such programmatic distortion:

> In truth . . . they [the prophets] have misled my people, saying
> "Peace" when there is no peace; . . . when the people build a wall,
> these prophets smear whitewash on it. (Ezek. 13:10)

These recognized voices of established reality deliberately misrepresent the true state of the economy and of foreign policy. Society has broken down and is not working, and they legitimate the dysfunction and give false assurance. The voices of accepted legitimacy present a fake reality, with failed fact disguised as workable fantasy. The prophetic traditions accepted as canonical are agreed that such fantasy will bring devastation upon a deceived community.[6]

We have here made a large leap from face-to-face neighborliness into the royal engine room of public distortion. With this leap, I may suggest three facets of "false witness" that invite to killing distortion. These distortions in our contemporary world echo those against whom the great prophets railed.

1. *Euphemism.* The use of euphemism consists in describing a reality by labeling it in terms that completely disguise and misrepresent. Long ago Isaiah had noted the capacity to deceive by giving things false names:

> Ah, you who call evil good
> and good evil,
> who put darkness for light
> and light for darkness,
> who put bitter for sweet
> and sweet for bitter! (Isa. 5:20)[7]

Those who control the media have vast opportunity for such sustained intentional distortion. Robert Lifton has chronicled the way in which the perpetration of the Jewish Shoah cast these deathly operations in "toxic euphemisms," so that the entire process of the death camps could be presented as a practice of medicine.[8]

In our own time, moreover, Noam Chomsky has characterized the ways in which the public apparatus is endlessly submissive to deliberate misnomer.[9] The deceiving work of euphemism—which is a public pattern of false witness against neighbor—is especially effective in two areas of our common life. First the entire military industry and the so-called defense program of the world's last superpower are regularly disguised by euphemism, for the simple reason that a massive killing enterprise to protect inequity in the world dare not be called by its right name. This is evident in giving peaceable names for missiles capable of massive destruction. Second, in like manner, the rapacious free-market economy delights in euphemism, in order to cover over the human pain and cost of extraordinary and unconscionable profits. Thus, as Chomsky notes, unemployment becomes "down-sizing," "jobs" has now become a four-letter word for "profit," and greed operates under the name of "opportunity."

2. The capacity for misrepresentation is especially poignant in television *advertising*,[10] which posits a never-never land born in the happy ways of the "product." In that land there is never pain, never hurt, never fear, never poverty, never any negation that is not overcome by "the product." One would not ever know from such ads that the gaps between rich and poor grow like a cancer in our society. The ads present a "virtual reality" enormously attractive but remote from where the world must be lived.

3. Closely related to advertising is the incredible world of *propaganda*, which offers a vested interest as a totality of truth, which generates false certitudes and false loyalties that belie the reality of human life.[11]

The church, in its accommodating timidity, has characteristically wanted to keep the commandments of Sinai safely in modest zones of moralizing. It is unmistakable, however, that *euphemism, advertising,* and *propaganda* all serve to bear false witness against neighbor. And since dominant "word-making" and "world-making" are always in the hands of those who control technology, these pseudo-versions of reality are regularly the work of the strong against the weak, the haves against the have-nots. The consequence is to make invisible and unavailable the truth of life in the world.

III

The rhetoric of the courtroom operates where "truth" is unsettled, in dispute, and still to be determined. The ancient agrarian prohibition against false witness seeks to stop social distortions that make life brutal, exploitative, and unbearable. Against these propensities, the prophets urge that the deathly truth of the world must be told, a truth that characteristically lives and works at the expense of the weak.

Along with *the truth of the world,* this commandment concerns *telling the truth about God.* This may seem so obvious as not to warrant comment. Except that "God" is completely enmeshed in social-political-economic realities.[12] In order to maintain social advantage, it is often necessary to tell the truth about God in false ways, because the "really real," that is, the gospel truth about God, is revolutionary, subversive, and disruptive.

In Second Isaiah, we may see how this simple agrarian prohibition is now turned into a theological agenda whereby Yahweh is "the Neighbor" about whom the truth must be told. Israel must bear true witness to this Neighbor in the midst of exile. Some exiled Jews, apparently, had come to terms with Babylonian realities, accepted the legitimacy of Babylonian gods, and engaged in Babylonian modes of life. That is, the claims of God had to be conformed—by false witnesses—to power realities. The prophet critiques "the witnesses" who submit to "idols" that can neither see nor hear nor do anything (Isa. 44:9). Those false gods to whom false witness is given generate false lived reality.

The poet seeks to counter that entire cache of falseness by a summons to truth-telling. Israel is to tell the truth about Yahweh, to be Yahweh's true witnesses:

> Do not fear, or be afraid;
> have I not told you from of old and declared it?
> *You are my witnesses!*
> Is there any god besides me?
> There is no other rock; I know not one. (Isa. 44:8; emphasis mine)

In the preceding chapter, Yahweh also asserts to the exiled Jews: "You are my witnesses" (43:10). And the testimony to be given concerns Yahweh's capacity to initiate an alternative in the world, to work a newness in society, to emancipate Israel, and to overcome the military-industrial power and hubris of Babylon. When true witness is given to this awesome Neighbor, it is about rescue, liberation, and transformation:

> I, I am the Lord,
> and besides me there is no savior.
> I declared and saved and proclaimed,
> when there was no strange god among you
> and you are my witnesses,
> says the Lord.
> I am God, and also henceforth I am He;
> there is no one who can
> deliver from my hand;
> I work and who can hinder it? . . .
> Thus says the Lord,
> who makes a way in the sea,
> a path in the mighty waters,
> who brings out chariot and horse.
> army and warrior; . . .
> I am about to do a new thing;
> now it springs forth,
> do you not perceive it? (Isa. 43:11-13, 16-17, 19)

The truth about Yahweh is that Yahweh is about to disrupt and make a newness. If Israel tells falsehood about Yahweh, then Yahweh will be weak, passive, and impotent, yet another adornment of the status quo. This truth or falsehood about this holy, magisterial Neighbor is not a cognitive matter of having the right "idea." It is rather a practical, concrete matter of voicing the authority, energy, and legitimacy of living a liberated life and thereby going home. False or true witness concerns the actual future of life in the world. Those who are "kept" and domesticated by Babylon may lie about Yahweh. Those prepared for Yahweh's alternative future, however, tell the truth, which causes the dismantling of the powers of alienation and death, powers which thrive only on falsehood.

IV

When this ancient agrarian prohibition is made larger and more public by the prophets and then is carried into the New Testament, the requirement of *telling the truth about God* devolves into *telling the truth about Jesus*. The Fourth Gospel, like Second Isaiah, is cast in juridical rhetoric in order to make an argument and stage a dispute about the true character of Jesus. In this regard, Israel is not to bear false witness against its Neighbor, and the church is not to bear false witness against Jesus.[13]

In the Fourth Gospel, John the Baptizer is the forerunner of Jesus to whom witness is first of all made:

> You yourselves are my witnesses that I said, "I am not the Messiah." (John 3:28)

The same rhetoric is employed by Jesus:

> If I testify about myself, my testimony is not true. There is another who testifies on my behalf, and I know that his testimony to me is true. You sent messengers to John, and he testified to the truth. . . . But I have a testimony greater than John's. The works that the Father has given me to complete, the very works that I am doing, testify on my behalf that the Father has sent me. And the Father who sent me has himself testified on my behalf. (John 5:31, 32, 36-37)

The Fourth Gospel is presented as a dispute about the truth of Jesus. The assertion and vindication of that truth concerns the character of Jesus, his relation to his Father, and his crucifixion and resurrection.

The Fourth Gospel apparently culminates in the "trial of Jesus," or better, "the trial of Pilate."[14] Before the Roman governor, Jesus asserts:

> For this I was born, and for this I came into the world, to testify to the truth. (18:37)

And Pilate hauntingly responds:

> What is truth? (v. 38)

What indeed! The Gospel narrative is notoriously enigmatic. But surely it makes a claim, certainly in its own idiom, that in Jesus of Nazareth the things of the world are settled on God's terms. That is the truth before which the Roman governor stands in dismay.

The world—the recalcitrant world presided over by the Roman governor—cannot bear the truth of Jesus, for that truth moves beyond our capacity to control and our power to understand. And so the world "gives false witness" about Jesus. In doing so, it gives false representation about the world. Just as exilic Jews preferred not to tell the truth about Yahweh because it is a truth too subversive, so many of us in the church choose to bear false witness about Jesus, because the managed, reassuring truth of the empire is more compelling. The truth evidenced in Jesus is not an idea, not a concept, not a formulation, not a fact. It is rather a way of being in the world in suffering and hope, so radical and so raw that we can scarcely entertain it.

V

Telling *the truth about God*, telling *the truth about Jesus*, and telling *the truth about the world* are intimately connected to each other. They are intimately connected in the Sinai covenant whereby God asserts a powerful relation to the world: "The whole earth is mine" (Exod. 19:5). They are even more visibly linked in the life of Jesus, wherein the purposes of God take fleshly form. Conversely, it is inescapably the case that lying about God, lying about Jesus, and lying about the world are inextricably related to each other.

We have learned to lie well:[15]

- We imagine that God is not the bestirrer of radical newness.
- We conclude that the suffering of Jesus is not our redemptive vocation.
- We assert that the world—and our economy—is all fine, fine on its own terms with imperial gods and a pliable Jesus.

We, even with our resolved faith, tend to live inside that reassuring ideology that can recognize nothing deathly and that can receive nothing new.

The world of the Bible consists of a dispute about evidence. The baptized community is "in the dock," summoned to tell the truth and not to bear false witness. The preacher, moreover, is regularly and visibly put on exhibit, to tell the church's truth to the world and to tell God's truth to the church. Very often the world refuses to hear, and of course the church is regularly recalcitrant in receiving testimony. And even the preacher, on occasion, cringes from what must be said, so much are we ourselves accommodated to "the lie."

We can admit all of that. And yet! And yet preaching goes on, folks gather, waiting fearfully but also hopefully for another witness that tells the whole truth. And so, good preacher, we may acknowledge the pressure and the way we flinch. But there is also the enduring possibility: Truth in dispute, and our feeble utterance to be sure that our Neighbor is rightly offered and discerned.

The truth now to be told concerns our failed society:

> Political power is now firmly in the hands of the money power in a symbiotic relationship that feeds inequity and injustice. Wealth is derived from power. And power in America is exercised almost exclusively by the wealthy.[16]

The prophets know this, and cannot call it "peace." But there is more. The gods of death have pushed hard on Friday. But faithful testimony requires a Sunday "bulletin" that expresses our amazement against the Friday forces of our life.

I am no romantic. I know this explosiveness of Easter that exposes all "prior" truths as false witnesses cannot be said in many churches. The wonder is that it is available to us. It is a truth we not only fear but also crave. Happily some in the church besides us preachers already know. Truthtelling is not easy work. But it is freeing. And it is the only defense the neighborhood has, both our *lower-case "n" neighbors* and our *capital "N" Neighbor*. And we are invited to take no bribes!

8

"Placeδ" between Promise
anδ Commanδ

I

T<small>HE LAND AS ISRAEL'S PLACE IS UNDERSTOOD FIRST OF ALL AS A GIFT FROM</small>
God. Thus the very first words uttered in the text by God to this "family of
Israel" are the words spoken by God to father Abraham:

> Go from your country and your kindred and your father's house to
> the land that I will show you. (Gen. 12:1)

It is decisive for Israel's understanding of itself and of its place that narrative memory begins with the speech of God, suggesting that there is a transcendent element in Israel's origin and destiny. The speech takes the form of
a promise, a promise that persists through the life of Israel and in the face
of every circumstance.

But the reception of the land promise only has effectiveness within the
ongoing relationship between giver and receiver. This promise is one of the
major affirmations of the Bible concerning place: the matrix of having a
place is intimately linked to having a right relationship with the promise-
maker.

II

The high theological claim of promise does not override the Bible's readiness to be realistic about the land. When Israel arrived, there were already
other, non-Israelite folk there who regarded the land as their own, and who
did not easily accept Israel's religious claim of a land grant from God. Thus
already in Gen. 12:6, just verses after the defining promise of Gen. 12:1-3,
we are told, "At that time, the Canaanites were in the land." The presence
of others in the land is a primary fact of Israel's life.

Now since all of these peoples go by the name of "Canaanite," and since
their presence is a great vexation to Israel, we may reflect more upon the
significance of this presence. There is a rough scholarly consensus that the
term "Canaanite" is not an ethnic term when it is used in Israel's land traditions, and even the formulary "seven nations" (Deut. 7:1, Judg. 3:1-5) is
not used with any precision. Rather the term "Canaanite" is a pejorative
code word used to refer to modes of public power and social relationships
that are exploitative and oppressive.[1] Or in Israel's frame of reference,
"Canaanite" means "anti-covenantal," or we may say "anti-neighborly."
The "Canaanites" are the "other" to Israel who are seen to constitute a

99

threat (putting Israel's place at risk) or a seduction (persuading Israel to abandon its covenantal vision of the land). While this antithetical mode of social organization signalled by the term "Canaanite" does not justify all the violence present in Israel's land tradition, it does help us understand why Israel concluded that Canaanite systems of land management must be eliminated, if the land of promise was to be a land of neighborliness.

Given the presence of such previous owners who were still present and claiming to be the continuing owners of the land, Israel had very limited options. First, Israel could assume an adversarial relation with those occupants, reflected in Judg. 1:28, 30, 33, 34; 2:3. Second, Israel had the option of peaceful coexistence, as is reflected in Judg. 1:29, 32. Thus in ancient Israel the wondrous theological claim of God's promise and gift is held in acute tension with the practical reality of displacement and usurpation. The biblical text suggests that ancient Israel was not unmindful of, nor at ease about, this always open and unresolved question.

III

The land of promise to which Israel came was organized in "Canaanite" ways. That is not to say that the "Canaanites" were "evil," but only that the land was organized in the conventional ways of the world, so that society consisted in "big ones" and "little ones," in "haves" and "have-nots." While the land may have been organized into urban dwellers and agrarian peasants (or semi-nomads), in fact the urban power structure had all the power and regularly confiscated the produce of the agrarian peasants for their own benefit.

While some other observer might imagine this was all quite "normal," the Israelites—fresh from the covenant-making of Mt. Sinai and the social vision of Moses—discerned these "normal" practices to be untenable, even if well-established and conventionally accepted as legitimate. Indeed, it is this Sinai-Moses tradition of covenant and commandment that propels biblical faith and that endlessly champions "a more excellent way" in the neighborhood. Thus even in the face of entrenched power relations, visionary voices in Israel relentlessly insisted upon that "more excellent way" in social relationships.

The book of Deuteronomy, which purports to be the teaching of Moses, stands as the great covenantal alternative to "Canaanite" modes of production and ownership. The book of Deuteronomy holds passionately to the great conviction that the "land of Canaan" is transformable and is indeed open to change.

There are two themes in the long address of Moses in Deuteronomy. First, Moses perceives that the Canaanite modes of social order are so effective and attractive that they constitute a threat to Israel. There is a chance that Israel will be so attracted to (seduced by) Canaanite ways of arranging power, that is, exploitatively, that Israel will forget that the land is a gift demanding faith, and that the land is an arena for the practice of neighborly covenanting. That is, Israel may abandon its very reason for existence, and simply disappear into the conventional economics of the land. Moses pauses so long in order to warn, caution, and admonish Israel that Israel should not be talked out of its peculiar vision of what its place should look like.

But there is also a second reason Moses pauses so long at the Jordan. Not only did Moses view the Canaanite-shaped land of promise as a threat and a seduction that jeopardized Israel's vision of social reality. The long-talking Moses of Deuteronomy also believed that this "distorted" land of promise, distorted by exploitative social relationships, did not need to stay that way, but could be transformed. That is, the people of Israel, when powered and energized by an intentional vision, can indeed change their place and make it a livable, life-giving place. This is a remarkable faith claim that has been decisive for Western culture. The "place" is not fated but can be brought to an alternative destiny by the intentionality of the new vision-driven inhabitants. The land as a social reality, that is, not simply as a one-dimensional piece of real estate, takes on a different quality, depending upon the attitude, conduct, and policies of its inhabitants. Places depend upon the kind of people who inhabit them and take on the character of their occupants.

The particular strategy of Moses concerning the transformation of the land is to insist that the vision of covenantal social relationships whereby the strong and the weak, the "haves" and "have-nots" share a common destiny, is to be enacted by obedience to covenantal commands. That is, Israel's sense of place requires that the place be "managed," not by convenience or by conventional common sense or by the enactment of vested interest, but by commands that call for quite intentional covenantal behavior. It is the commands that link together large visionary possibility and local, daily practice. Or in the parlance of Moses, the "will of God" is linked to the claims of neighborliness. This remarkable conviction holds together affirmations that we tend to split apart. Who would have thought that the "God of gods and Lord of lords" would have to fend off bribes or would provide food or clothing for the needy? Who would imagine that it is the vision of God that issues in the social imperative about caring for needy strangers? Moses' insistence is that how the neighborhood is ordered is related to Israel's largest vision of reality, that is, its vision of God.

Moses, however, does not settle for such a general rhetorical appeal. The appeal is followed and detailed by concrete commands, that is, rules for conduct in Israel's new place:

1. *Deuteronomy 15:1-11*.[2] Every society has creditors and debtors, so that social relationships have an inescapable economic component, a dimension of social reality that makes for easy exploitation. In that ancient society,

those who could not pay their debts eventually ended up as indentured workers, that is, as debt-slaves working only to pay off mortgages. They were then what we might now call a "permanent underclass." Moses proposes that this underclass status of indenture is not to be permanent in Israel, because Israel anticipates a different quality of social place. The command requires that the indebted person can only be kept in a position of dependence, coercion, and humiliation for a period of six years. After six years the debt, if it cannot be paid, is to be cancelled. Economic relations are understood as a subset of the social fabric, which has larger purposes that preempt and override economic claims. Thus debt is not an ultimate determinant of social relations, for in fact the provision of the command undermines the viability of any conventional economics.

The commandment, however, does not simply entail forgiveness of a debt. It provides that the indentured worker, when released with debts cancelled, shall not be sent destitute back into the economy. Rather the creditor shall not be "hard-hearted or tight-fisted toward your needy neighbor" (v. 7). The creditor is required to "willingly lend" (v. 8) or "give liberally and ungrudgingly" (v. 10). Thus the command concerns the capacity of the indebted to reenter the economy with dignity, self-respect, and viability, through neighborly care.

Moreover, while the command is famous (through the reference made to it by Jesus in Mark 14:7) that "there will never cease to be some in need in the earth" (v. 11), the command envisions that there will "be no one in need among you" (v. 4). This command anticipates not simply modest acts of charity and compassion, but a major transformation of economics whereby poverty is eradicated in a community that handles its wealth in genuinely neighborly ways. The radicality of this core provision can hardly be overstated. Indeed, the healthy transformation of Israel's place requires a break with both a conventional market economy and a state economy. Moses anticipates an economy of neighbors, a practice that pertains for Israel not only in a simple face-to-face economy but in every attempt to establish viable community.

2. *Deuteronomy 17:14-20*. Moses in Deuteronomy is also about the daring business of devising and authorizing new social institutions and practices as new social need arises. New social reality requires new modes of power and administration. Chief among these new modes is the institution of monarchy. The monarchy as a form of centralized power was unknown in early "egalitarian" Israel and represented what some viewed as a major distortion of Israel's common life.

Given the inescapable emergence of centralized power in the form of kingship, however, Moses concedes nothing in this command to conventional forms of exploitative, centralized power. The form of monarchy is accepted by Moses, but the conventional substance of kingship is roundly refused. The peculiar form of royal power envisioned by Moses is a practice of power that does not override neighborliness. Thus the proposed king must not multiply for himself silver and gold (that is, inordinate wealth), horses or chariots (that is, armaments), or wives (that is, political alliances arranged through marriage). That is, social power in Israel is to avoid all the distortions of neighborliness that are routine in "Canaanite" society.

There is, so says Moses, an important alternative to such exploitative conventions. Instead of personal aggrandizement, this king is to spend his days of power reading the Torah and pondering the distinctive memory and identity of Israel. The king is to reflect endlessly upon his true placement in an ongoing community of obedience, liberation, and covenant. Moses clearly believes and insists that Israel's public, structured, institutional life can be made congenial to and supportive of equitable, just social relations.

What Moses requires for the institution of monarchy is also required for other necessary social institutions, such as judges (17:8-13), prophets (18:9-22), priests (18:1-8), and cities of refuge (19:1-13).[3] Israel is free to appropriate conventional social practices but in each case must recharacterize and revise such social practice in ways appropriate to its own social passion and social vision.

3. *Deuteronomy 19:14.* This terse command on "boundary markers" provides none of the rhetorical appeal or flourish of the other commands we have considered. Nonetheless, it is equally crucial for Israel's covenantal notion of place. It recognizes that each member of the community must have a safe, unthreatened place (property) that will be respected and guaranteed by the acknowledgement of all the other neighbors. It further recognizes that the maintenance of good neighborly relations does not depend upon the capacity to defend forcibly one's personal place, but upon the coherence of the community, which recognizes and accepts the legitimacy of the place of the other.

It is clear that this simple command has importance and force in more complex social relations as well. Specifically, Prov. 23:10-11 sees that the ancient land marker that is endangered is the land marker of an orphan, that is, a vulnerable person who in a patriarchal society has lost the male advocate who will defend that right. The mention of orphan, one socially vulnerable, suggests that even the simple command of Deut. 19:14 is concerned with the threat of excessive power whereby the strong can preempt the legitimate interests of the weak. Thus the moving of boundary markers may not concern the simple act of moving a post. It may be the much more complex and sophisticated action of smart lawyers and foreclosing banks, and in more public matters the exercise of the right of "eminent domain," which gives the strong legal ways to seize land for their own purposes. Thus, for example, the rural prophet Micah warns against land operators who

> covet fields, and seize them;
> houses, and take them away,

> they oppress household and house,
> people and their inheritance. (Mic. 2:2)

The tale of Naboth's vineyard (1 Kings 21) is an example of eminent domain whereby a vulnerable citizen is denied his patrimony by the operation of a royal theory of land.

Thus the command of 19:14 concerns not only land management, but the ways in which economic activity is situated without social relations that must be honored, even if they curb the free activity of market forces. Israel's simplicity of expression must not beguile us, so that we do not notice the determined and demanding social vision that operates within such a seemingly simple statement.

4. *Deuteronomy 20:19-20; 22:6-7.* These two laws appear to be quite incidental to the teaching of Moses, and have not been much noticed. The former has been mostly considered only in terms of an understanding of war, and the latter has been studied almost not at all. As a result of recent ecological awareness, however, in these two laws we are able to see an inchoate, but nonetheless important, concern for the ecology of the land.

Deuteronomy 20:19-20 occurs at the conclusion of a long chapter of provisions about the waging of war. As everyone knows, war devastates the natural environment where it is conducted. In part this is because of the actual work of combat. But it is also because of utilizing natural resources as material for combat. In that ancient world, a major military tactic was siege (for example, 2 Sam. 12:26-31), for which great timber was required. Because the passions of war seem to override every other social concern, the timbers for siege are taken, no matter the cost.

In such a context, the command of Moses is remarkable. The utilization of timber for siege weapons is permitted, but within an important limitation. Israel is permitted to take only trees that "do not produce food," that is, fruit trees. In a quite indirect way, this text recalls the lyrical affirmation of fruitfulness in the creation narrative of Gen. 1:11, 29. The creation is intended for fruitfulness, the production of life. And that fruitfulness intended for the creation is the irreducible first reality of all social relations. The maintenance of fruitfulness that can work and fulfill its proper function is the first human obligation. Nothing must interfere with that irreducible first reality, not state necessity, not the passions of war, not hate or revenge, not the love of violence or rapacious greed. Thus a purpose larger than human conflict sets a limit upon the range of human conflict, and the legitimate appetite of human control and expansion.

In a less dramatic way, Deut. 22:6-7 sounds a like affirmation. This command presents a more domestic scene, a walk in the woods. Upon finding a bird's nest with eggs in it and the mother bird with the eggs, one may be tempted to seize both the eggs and the mother bird. One may be tempted to do so to get food, or simply out of curiosity. Moses, however, sorts out matters very closely. The eggs may be taken, but not the mother bird. Because the mother bird is the agent of fruitfulness, and an Israelite may not disrupt the food chain upon which everyone depends. Israel knows that rapacious acts such as killing a mother bird will disrupt the earth's work of fruitfulness and in principle will make the earth inhospitable and finally unlivable.

These commands intend to curb the "Canaanite" temptation to self-sufficiency and self-aggrandizement, whereby one is free to do whatever one wants to do. These commands insist that all social acts in Israel (economic transactions, institution building, respect for neighbor, and respect for earth) situate would-be autonomous acts in a matrix of relations that concern neighborliness, which is situated in the very fabric of creation. Every act has a moral shape to it that cannot be violated without great harm and long-range destructive consequences. Moses insists that the most specific daily act be understood in terms of its inescapable, long-term moral shape.

IV

Because the land is both promised to Israel and occupied by others, because the land is both a threat to faith and a possible arena of transformation, because the land is saturated with large, public ethical issues, Israel understands that its life in the land is a vulnerable enterprise, freighted with danger and possibility.

On the one hand, it is promised that Israel can indeed keep the land, if Israel attends to the neighborly dimension of social reality in the land. Thus Israel's rhetoric is filled with buoyant expectations, anticipating long life in the land through many generations. The commands that make life in the land possible are not burdensome but simply are the normal and inescapable markings of viable community life. Thus it is promised that "you may live long in the land [God has given you]" (Deut. 5:33; cf. 8:1; 11:9, 21, 16:20; 25:15). All of these assurances and possibilities are set within the context of command. Attachment to this God-given place, which is safe, fruitful, and productive (that is, blessed), is indeed conditional. Israel, in the book of Deuteronomy and more generally in its rhetoric of commitment, resolves to keep the conditions and accept the land on the terms of covenant (cf. Exod. 24:3, 7; Josh. 24:21, 24-25). The condition is neighborliness which is the only way to keep a place.

On the other hand, Israel in its most candid reflection knows that it can lose the land. It will lose the land if it disregards the commands, if it acts as though it were autonomous and self-sufficient and free to use the land for its own greedy purposes. The promise of God to give the land does not pertain to land that is held in foolish ways, that is, without regard to neighborliness.

Thus Israel is warned that "you will . . . utterly perish from the land" (Deut. 4:26; cf. 8:19-20; 11:17; 28:20, 22). The notion of perishing is carefully nuanced. The disappearance of Israel will happen through long-term natural processes. These may include drought (Deut. 11:17) or a host of pathologies (28:20-22). Or perishing may mean that the Israelite vision of neighborliness is forfeited, and by their greedy lack of caring, the Israelites disappear into the landscape of Canaanite exploitation. And then it will be as though the Exodus of liberation had never happened, and Israel finds itself again brutally enmeshed in old patterns of oppressiveness and despair.

Thus Israel's sense of place concerns a deep either/or about the command that guarantees the promise. We should be clear, however, that the command is not an imposition of legalism, as though Moses (or God) were cranky or coercive. Rather the command is Israel's distinctive way in which to speak about the irreducible reality that healthy place requires healthy social relationships. This conditionality cannot be circumvented by power, knowledge, or wealth, for it is intrinsic to the land process itself. The neighbor is the irreducible condition of healthy, peaceable, productive place.

We may cite two poignant articulations of this uncompromising either/or. In Deut. 8:17-20, Moses draws a sharp contrast between remembering and forgetting. Remembering (v. 18) concerns the palpable awareness that God gives power to get wealth and that power and wealth are covenantal operations. Forgetting (v. 19) is the scuttling of the awareness of God, the disregard of covenanting, and the perverted imagination of self-sufficiency that "my power and the might of my own hand have gotten me this wealth" (v. 17). This latter deception of autonomy will lead to placelessness (v. 20).

Deuteronomy 30:15-20 presents the same issue of promise and command as a choice of life and death that concerns the embrace of the commands of neighboring. The language is intensely theological, that is, it concerns a choice of gods. The choice of gods, however, is not intellectual, theoretical, or cognitive. It is a quite concrete practical matter. Israel chooses Yahweh (or another god) not by theological verbiage, but by the way it treats indentured servants, by the way it orders centralized power, by the way it respects boundary markers, and by the way it treats fruit trees and mother birds.

One does not therefore need to be a militant theological type to see that Israel's sense of place is not outmoded or obsolete for our own time. The issues that confronted Moses in Deuteronomy are the same issues that confront a complex postindustrial, urban society. Either the neighbor is honored, respected, and cared for in terms of social policy and social practice, or deep human losses and pathologies arise that threaten us all. As Moses understood so well, there is no escape from this either/or, not by might, not by wealth, not by technological sophistication.

V

As ancient Israel tells its story, the community chose death. It found the condition of neighborliness too demanding and too inconvenient. Thus the classic account of Israel's life under the monarchy (in Joshua, Judges, 1 and 2

Samuel, 1 and 2 Kings) is a narrative interpretation of the way in which disregard of command led to exile, displacement, and disarray (cf. 1 Kings 9:4-7).

The telling of this tale in the Hebrew Bible/Old Testament ends in exile, as though death and losing the land have fully prevailed over life and keeping the land. That is on the whole where the narrative account focuses.

That descriptive account, however, has set alongside it a visionary alternative. It took the courageous prophets and daring poets of Israel to move past the terrible either/or of Deut. 30:15-20 and 1 Kings 9:4-7, to suggest there was a way for this community beyond the death of anti-neighborliness which had been chosen.

No voicing of this alternative is more eloquent than is Ezek. 37:1-14. The prophet must employ a most daring and radical image in order to speak about a return to the land and a new possibility for life in the land. Such an extreme articulation is required, because such a possibility moves against the experienced reality of land loss. Israel could hardly believe that restoration to the land was possible, and therefore the prophet must use images that violate all the weary conventions of Israel's despair. Thus Ezekiel speaks about resurrection:

> I open your graves, and bring you up from your graves, O my people. (v. 13)

It is clear, however, that this speech about resurrection is for the prophet a metaphor. The next verse explicates the metaphor:

> I will place you on your own soil; then you shall know that I, the Lord, have spoken and will act, says the Lord. (v. 14)

Israel will begin again, "on your own soil," the very piece of land long since promised. What makes this second choice possible after the first choice has been forfeited is that "I will put my spirit within you" (v. 14). It is the spirit-wind-power of God that blows in and through old deathly choices, that permits Israel yet again to redecide for its life in its place. It is this redeciding that is required for a place, even if old deathly choices are still an option and a temptation.

Moses invited Israel to stand firm in its peculiar and distinctive notion of place. Between the free gift and promise and the condition of command, Israel knows that its place is at the same time its very own and not its own. It cannot scuttle the moral reality of place, cannot scuttle the God who promises and commands, cannot scuttle the neighbor who looms large just across the boundary.

Israel is peculiar in its sense of place. It offers itself persistently as a way whereby others can learn something decisive and inescapable about being in the right place. To be well placed means to listen and to care. Not listening and not caring constitute a terrible alternative for Israel, or for anyone else.

9

The Truth of Abundance:
Relearning Dayenu

THE CHURCH HAS BEEN THINKING ABOUT FOOD SINCE ITS BEGINNING WHEN Jesus had compassion on the crowd, feeding 5,000 with twelve baskets-full left over (Mark 6:30-44) and then 4,000 with seven baskets-full left over (Mark 8:1-10). It is always a crowd *without bread* and Jesus strangely *giving bread*. Long before the church, Israel has been thinking about food for a very long time. This is the community that left the "fleshpots" of Egypt and found themselves hungry in the wilderness, and then food came wondrously from heaven and they said "What is it?"—which in the Hebrew is *man-hû'*. But of course long before Israel or the church, every creature in God's world, human and nonhuman, had been thinking about food, because food is the most elemental requirement, close to the most elemental satisfaction, and the most elemental sacramental mediation of significant humanness to any of us. From long before the royal families of the world had cake, the human community had wanted bread, had eaten bread, had treasured bread, and had shared bread.

Since all of you are already "true believers," my task is not to say anything new, but to outline what we all believe passionately. I plan to do this from my own reflection and research, outlining something of the history of food in the Bible.

1

The beginning point in the Bible, for Israel and for the world, is of course God. The beginning point for God, so the Bible asserts, is the wonder and goodness of creation. It is not necessary to get caught in such matters as "religion and science" or "creation and evolution." In the Bible, "creation" is primarily an exuberant, lyrical, doxological expression of gratitude and amazement for the goodness and generosity of God. The theme that recurs is *generosity and abundance*. There is enough! There is more than enough! There is as much as the limitless, self-giving of God can imagine.

And so already in Genesis! Israel's opening doxology in Gen. 1 affirms that God is endlessly generous and has created a world of fruitfulness and productivity. God has arranged the world, all creatures, all sea monsters, all creeping things, all animals, all plants, each according to its kind. And God has decreed, "bring forth, bring forth, bear fruit, produce, multiply, generate." The radishes and wheat and rabbits and frogs and eels and hedgehogs are all like first graders who blossom when they see the teacher. They work harder and in so doing, they become their true selves. And so all the creatures delight to please their creator and seek to produce, and in so doing become their true selves. Israel is endlessly astonished at the wonder of the food chain.

The wonder at the food supply is expressed in Israel's singing. So in Psalm 104, a wondrous doxological inventory reflects on the gift of food:

> You cause the grass to grow for the cattle,
> and plants for people to use,
> to bring forth food from the earth,
> and wine to gladden the human heart,
> oil to make the face shine,
> and bread to strengthen the human heart.
> The trees of the Lord are watered abundantly,
> the cedars of Lebanon that he planted.
> In them the birds build their nests;
> the stork has its home in the fir trees.
> The high mountains are for the wild goats;
> the rocks are a refuge for the coneys.
> You have made the moon to mark the seasons;
> the sun knows its time for setting.
> You make darkness, and it is night,
> when all the animals of the forest come creeping out.
> The young lions roar for their prey,
> seeking their food from God.
> When the sun rises, they withdraw
> and lie down in their dens.
> People go out to their work
> and to their labor until the evening. (vv. 14-23)

The inventory ends with a great exclamation:

> O Lord, how manifold are your works!
> In wisdom you have made them all;
> the earth is full of your creatures. (v. 24)

And then something like a table prayer:

> These all look to you
> to give them their food in due season;
> when you give it to them,
> they gather it up;
> when you open your hand,
> they are filled with good things. (vv. 27-28)

Indeed table prayers thank for food; pauses for grace are our best practice of creation theology that celebrates the generosity of God. The same prayer is echoed in Psalm 145:

> The eyes of all look to you,
> and you give them their food in due season.
> You open your hand,
> satisfying the desire of every living thing. (vv. 15-16)

Israel reflects on the free gift of food: the earth germinates, the seasons work, water, sunshine, breeding, production, nurture, availability. It is a guaranteed system culminating in the food chain for those in God's image, the whole designed for us. There is the elemental generosity at the root of our human life in God's world. There is enough. Israel sings its *lyrics of abundance.*

II

As we know in our own time, it is not quite like that in the world. It is not quite like that in the Bible, either. Something has happened to God's abundance so nicely celebrated in the doxologies of Israel. The community of Israel appears in the Bible only beginning in Genesis 12. In vv. 1-3, Abram and Sarai are summoned by God to a risky venture, and they go. But by v. 10, we are back to the theme of food:

> Now there was a famine in the land. So Abram went down to Egypt
> to reside there as an alien, for the famine was severe in the land.

We are told two things. There was a famine. Now it may be that a famine is a "natural occurrence." It just happened in the course of things. This text does not reflect on it, but takes the famine as a given; something is amiss in the generosity and abundance of the creator. But we are told a second thing. They went to Egypt. There was food in Egypt. Pharaoh always had a good supply of food, so that the people of faith submit to the people of food.

The text is not excessively reflective. It does not ponder why there is food in Egypt, except that it knows about the productivity of the Nile that had been entrusted to Pharaoh. The Bible is preoccupied with Egypt and with Pharaoh and comes to regard Pharaoh as the great antithesis of the will of the creator. It takes a while to get there in the Bible. But the story builds. I will mention three texts about "the Egyptian problem" in the Bible, for *Egypt* is at the center of *the food problem* in the Bible.

1. *Genesis 47.* In this text, Pharaoh decides to prepare against a future famine by centralized planning. He appoints as the head of the planning commission for food, Joseph. Joseph is a most ambiguous character, situated as he is between his people Israel and Pharaoh. In the end, however, he turns against his people and joins the Pharonic monopoly. How could he not! He is so clever and he understands the bureaucratic deployment of technology.

So we are told in the forty-seventh chapter of Genesis. The hungry came to Joseph for food, on which he had a monopoly. He gave them food and took their money. That is, he sold them food, no doubt at his own prices, for he had a monopoly. The famine lasted a long time, so they came to him for food a second year. They had no more cash, so he took their means of production: horses, flocks, herds, and donkeys. The third year they came to him for food, but they had no more money and no more livestock. But they implored the bureaucrat:

> Shall we die before your eyes, both we and our land? Buy us and our land in exchange for food. We with our land will become slaves to Pharaoh; just give us seed, so that we may live and not die, and that the land may not become desolate. (v. 19)

They sold themselves into bondage, to become state debt-slaves, a permanent underclass that would always be a year behind, working to pay off last year's food bill, surely at high interest rates, for the people with the food monopoly tend to determine the credit arrangements for the community.

Two conclusions are drawn from this ominous narrative. First:

> As for the people, he made slaves of them from one end of Egypt to the other. (v. 21)

Everyone now depended on the corporate monopoly. But second, there is an exception:

> Only the land of the priests he did not buy; for the priests had a fixed allowance from Pharaoh, and lived on the allowance that Pharaoh gave them; therefore they did not sell their land. (v. 22)

The imperial monopoly depended upon religious legitimation, so the priests received a tax allowance and exception, in exchange for cooperation with the monopolizing regime. That sort of policy is no doubt behind 12:10; "there was famine . . . . they went to Egypt."

2. The second Egypt-Pharaoh text is in Ezek. 29:3-6, in which God promises, against the empire:

> I am against you,
> Pharaoh king of Egypt,
> the great dragon sprawling
> in the mist of its channels,
> saying, "My Nile is my own;
> I made it for myself." . . .
> I will draw you up from your channels,
> with all the fish of your channels
> sticking to your scales.
> I will fling you into the wilderness,
> you and all the fish of your channels;
> you shall fall in the open field,
> and not be gathered and buried. . . .

Then all the inhabitants of Egypt shall know
that I am the Lord. (Ezek. 29:3-6)

Pharaoh boasted and bragged that he had made the Nile, owned it and
could use it for his own end. Pharaoh, neglecting the claims of the creator,
thought he was autonomous and could use food as he wanted, food as
weapon, food as an instrument of state policy, food produced by the Nile
that was a gift of the creator.

Pharaoh is the great monopolizer, the great hoarder, the great manipula-
tor. And so, in the prophetic oracle of Ezekiel, he is condemned by the creator, caught like a fish on a hook and thrown into the wilderness, because
you cannot mock the creator of abundance by monopolizing the food production of creation and creating artificial scarcity.

3. The third Egypt-Pharaoh text is better known. In Exodus 1, Pharaoh
has become autonomous, greedy, and brutalizing. It goes with having a
monopoly. The monopoly grows more brutal, and then our mothers and
fathers in faith discovered:

The Egyptians became ruthless in imposing tasks on the Israelites,
and made their lives bitter with hard service in mortar and brick
and in every kind of field labor. They were ruthless in all the tasks
that they imposed on them. (Exod. 1:13-14)

Indeed, Pharaoh went crazy in his monopoly, so crazy that he decreed that
all slave-boys among the Hebrews should be killed and thrown into the
Nile. The Nile, the life-line of Egypt, has become a death canal! The strategy is like burning villages in Vietnam to save them. The channel of life is
now polluted by the brutality of death. I think the narrative in its ironic way
wants to assert that monopoly produces self-aggrandizement that eventually becomes insane and cuts off even the source of its own life.

Now if we are to understand the food crisis, in that ancient world or in
our own, we must pay close attention to what happens to Pharaoh and
what Pharaoh represents. The reality of drought or low production or
famine—whatever the cause—produces a sense of scarcity, a deep, fearful,
anxious conviction that there is not enough to go around, and that no more
will be given. The proper response, given that anxiety, is to keep everything
you have, to get good protection to keep what you have from others who
want it, to take steps to secure still more at the expense of others, more that
may belong to others, more than you need, more than you will ever need.
The *myth of scarcity* that can drive the economy is not based on economic
analysis but on anxiety. Such a drive for food—and more generally for security—requires both a reliable labor pool to do the chores of the state and a
parallel military apparatus to defend the inordinate supplies of the monopoly. Pharaoh had all of these.

I do not need to report to you that it is the myth of scarcity that drives
the modern economy and that controls the administration of food. It

occurred to me that during the recent disastrous earthquake in Iran, it would have been dazzling policy for the United States to overwhelm Iran with free food, an act that would have quickly transformed geopolitics. Except that we are restrained in our prosperous monopoly by the myth of scarcity.

The myth of scarcity is such an elemental power that we do not recognize or examine it. Douglas Meeks has written eloquently on the myth of scarcity, and I commend to you a recent book by Regina Schwartz, *The Curse of Cain*, that shows how the myth of scarcity produces sexual and ethnic violence in the Old Testament.[1] The myth of scarcity both produces and justifies violence against the neighbor.

In order to read biblical texts intelligently, we must of course ask, "Who now plays the role of Pharaoh?" The first answer, perhaps, is the United States as the last superpower, who administers the economic monopoly of which we are beneficiaries with our inordinate standard of living matched by our inordinate military mechanism. But it is argued by many recent scholars that the real monopolizing force in the world is not the U.S. government but it is the "money economy" driven by corporate power that recruits even the government as a company security force.[2] One can see the myth of scarcity at work in greedy CEO salaries, in obscene sports celebrity arrangements, in the general assumption of autonomous individualism, in so-called "welfare reform," in reduction of capital gains taxes, in all the drive to privatize wealth away from care for the public good. The myth of scarcity makes each an agent of acquisitiveness in the face of all the others who also pursue acquisitiveness.

My thesis is that a myth of scarcity will never generate "bread for the world," but only bread for us and for ours. And so I propose that the *lyric of abundance* that is evoked by the generosity of the creator, sits deep against the *myth of scarcity*. The lyric of abundance asserts that because the world is held in the hand of the generative, generous God, scarcity is not true. I mean this not as a pious, religious sentiment, but as a claim about the economy. The claim of creation faith is that there is more than enough to share, and where there is sharing there is generativity of more, because as the fruitful instruments of creation notice the *shalom* of God enacted as sharing, they do in fact produce more. Those of us who care about the lyric of abundance must reflect on whether we embrace this claim, and whether it is possible to break free from the claim of scarcity that is all around us, that is the dominant power of politics and the relentless liturgy of TV commercials.

III

This is not a new problem for our tradition of faith. People in our tradition of faith have endlessly struggled with a *departure from the myth of scarcity*, a liturgical, imaginative, political, economic act of resolve to situate our lives outside this powerful ideological claim. Did you notice I used the word "departure?" The Biblical word for departure is *Exodus*. Exodus is not just a geographical event. It is an economic act. It is an imaginative act, to begin to live without permitting the necessities of Pharaoh to dictate the circumstances of our life. Pharaoh, then and now, is endlessly powerful in his definitions of reality, and it is not easy to depart.

It is, however, the principle work of Israel in the ancient world to establish a *counter-practice* of life and faith that refuses, from the bottom up, the assumptions, claims, and persuasions of Pharaoh. Thus I imagine that Bread for the World stands in direct continuity with that ancient community of courage that sought to work out a food policy and a food practice congruent with its lyric of generosity and without reference to the fearful, mistaken, brutalizing notion of scarcity. I wish to identify a sequence of three steps in extricating creation faith from the power of Pharaoh.

1. Israel had to *leave Egypt* and its brutalizing definition of reality. That is what the Exodus story of Exodus 1–15 is all about. It is a dramatic narrative, endlessly reenacted for the sake of the children, about the confrontational contest, negotiation, bargaining, and trickery that contributed to the departure.

The slave community in its exploitation knew that Egyptian food practice, with all its abusive apparatus, was not right. No economic arrangement is right that causes so much suffering for so many people. They knew in their bones that it was not right; and the feeling in their bones was reinforced by the reality of God's holiness that came among them. The God of all holiness, the creator of abundance and generosity, does not will monopoly and does not accept scarcity as a rule of life. At the outset, Pharaoh has all the power, and Israel (under Moses) has none. The telling of the story, however, is the telling of how Moses and Israel and Yahweh slowly gain power and energy and courage and force, until they have the upper hand. In the end, Pharaoh, who is living a lie, is portrayed as a pitiful, weak suppliant who must beg Moses for a blessing, because he is no longer blessed (Exod. 12:32). This narrative perhaps is not more than street theater. But this community of an alternative food policy, in every generation, reenacts this confrontive narrative in order to be reminded that the myth of scarcity is a phony vision, and we must not give in to it.

God gave promises to this emerging community with its alternative food policy. God gave promises that outside Egypt, outside Egyptian definitions of reality, there is a another way to live. There is talk of "milk and honey," of the abundance intended by the creator. There is an order of well-being to which we are destined. And so they left!

2. When they left, they did not find themselves in the land flowing with milk and honey. Rather they found themselves in the wilderness, in a place where there did seem to be only scarcity. Our mothers and fathers, who

eagerly departed Egypt, were stunned at where they found themselves. They complained of poor leadership and rebelled:

> If only we had died by the hand of the Lord in the land of Egypt, when we sat by the fleshpots and ate our fill of bread; for you have brought us out into this wilderness to kill this whole assembly with hunger. (Exod. 16:3)

Their protest, vigorous as it is, is taken as a prayer. And the prayer is answered by God:

> In the evening quails came up and covered the camp; and in the morning there was a layer of dew around the camp. When the layer of dew lifted, there on the surface of the wilderness was a fine flaky substance, as fine as frost on the ground. When the Israelites saw it, they said to one another, "What is it?" For they did not know what it was. Moses said to them. "It is the bread that the Lord has given you to eat." (vv. 13-15)

This is a core miracle that happened in Exodus 16, just after the departure in Exodus 15. Bread from heaven is not given in Egypt. It is given in the wilderness, outside Egyptian definitions of what is possible, where there are no resources. The first task is leaving; the second task is *believing*. They are asked to believe that in the wilderness where the ground cannot generate food, food will be given from heaven in ways that are strange and inexplicable. Israel in the wilderness is brought face to face with the oddness of the creator who will give bread.

But the bread of heaven comes with the trademark requirement of Yahweh. There are instructions posted on the loaves:

> "Gather as much of it as each of you needs, an omer to a person according to the number of persons, all providing for those in their own tents." The Israelites did so, some gathering more, some less. But when they measured it with an omer, those who gathered much had nothing over, and those who gathered little had no shortage; they gathered as much as each of them needed. (vv. 16-18)

This is biblical rhetoric to mean "no hoarding." No storing up. Where there is no scarcity, there is no warrant for hoarding. No member of the community need be threatened by what the neighbor has, no need for greed, no need for brutality, no need for violence, no need for Pharaoh's way with bread, because Yahweh is the giver who keeps on giving, every day, sufficient for the day.

Israel's second task is believing, believing when you hold this fine flaky substance in your hand, that there will be more, believing that Yahweh is attentive as creator, that Yahweh is powerful in the desert, that Yahweh is unlike Pharaoh and so is perfectly reliable and perfectly generous.

It was not easy for Israel to believe in daily bread, as it is not easy for us, as we pray daily for bread. We are told:

> But they did not listen to Moses; some left part of it until morning, and it bred worms and became foul. And Moses was angry with them. Morning by morning they gathered it, as much as each needed; but when the sun grew hot, it melted. (vv. 20-21)

They had a miracle, but the miracle seemed to need some administrative finesse to assure its effectiveness. But such an extra day's supply begins the hoarding that ends in pharonic competition and conflict. So the bread for the day is fragile as well as flaky, requiring enormous trust as the only alternative to killing scarcity and to brutalizing monopoly.

3. After the courage to leave and the confidence to believe, they came to the land—finally. It was indeed a good land, as promised:

> And they came to the Wadi Eshcol, and cut down from there a branch with a single cluster of grapes, and they carried it on a pole between two of them. They also brought some pomegranates and figs. (Num. 13:23)

The good land is the fruition of the creation promise. It is visibly, concretely abundant!

But the entry into the land is no casual matter. It is one of the deep, critical moments in the history of faith, for everything has changed. During the wilderness time of Israel, the community depended on the generosity of heaven to give bread for the journey. But that wondrous daily bread, we are told, lasted only in the wilderness. Thus, in a pivotal assertion in the story of bread we are told:

> On the day after the passover, on that very day, they ate the produce of the land, unleavened cakes and parched grain. The manna ceased on the day they ate the produce of the land, and the Israelites no longer had manna; they ate the crops of the land of Canaan that year. (Josh. 5:11-12)

Now, instead of a generous heaven, they must rely on a productive earth. Instead of miracle, they are driven to agriculture. Instead of just receiving, they are now into management. And when Israel—or anybody—thinks about management, it will not be long before there are thoughts about property and ownership and self-sufficiency and greed, and we are back to all the circumstances that invite moves to monopoly and thoughts of scarcity.

The Bible is cunningly put together. Just after land entry in Joshua 5, only one story removed, there is the tale of Aachan in chapters 7–8. There was a terrible defeat in the community. When they investigated the problem (according to their primitive investigative methods), the evidence all pointed to Aachan as the transgressor whose handling of goods brought devastation on the community. Joshua addressees him:

> My son, give glory to the Lord God of Israel and make confession to him. Tell me now what you have done; do not hide it from me. (Josh. 7:19)

And Aachan answers readily:

> It is true; I am the one who sinned against the LORD God of Israel. This is what I did: when I saw among the spoil a beautiful mantle from Shinar, and two hundred shekels of silver, and a bar of gold weighing fifty shekels, then I coveted them and took them. They now lie hidden in the ground inside my tent, with the silver underneath. (vv. 20-21)

"I coveted them and I took them." He privatized community wealth. We learn two things. Coveting by a member of the community brings trouble on everyone. But more than that, we learn that *being in the land* generates *coveting*, no longer a willingness to live at risk, but a propulsion to secure one's own existence in selfish ways. The linkage of land/prosperity/coveting/ destructiveness is a new thing for Israel in the land of promise, the land of such rich possibility for ample bread.

V

After departing Egypt and after believing in the wilderness, Israel now comes to its third demanding food task, *sharing.* Israel's vision since Sinai, as an alternative to Egypt, is that everything must be shared, that if there is to be well-being in the community, all must have access. Those who have are bound in duty and in solidarity with those who do not have. Sharing in covenantal solidarity is what distinguishes Israel from the "atheists of scarcity" who turn neighbors into competitors for bread and finally into enemies with whom there must be endless wars for control of the bread supply.

The impetus for sharing bread is a key issue in the developing identity and vocation of Israel. I will mention three clusters of texts.

1. Moses, in the book of Deuteronomy, provides an ethic for the *land of prosperity*. It is the insistence of Moses that the land—and all of its resources—must be reorganized and reoriented for the sake of the community. But Moses singles out as a reference point three subgroups in the population: widows, orphans, undocumented workers—those without resources and without social leverage. The test of the community is its provision for the safety, dignity, and well-being of those who cannot secure their own food supply:

> The great God, mighty and awesome, who is not partial and takes no bribe, who executes justice for the orphan and the widow, and

who loves the strangers, providing them food and clothing. You
shall also love the stranger, for you were strangers in the land of
Egypt. (Deut. 10:17-19)
You shall bring out the full tithe of your produce for that year, and
store it within your towns; the Levites, because they have no allot-
ment or inheritance with you, as well as the resident aliens, the
orphans, and the widows in your town, may come and eat their fill
so that the Lord your God may bless you in all the work that you
undertake. (Deut. 14:28-29)
. . . when you have gathered in the produce from your threshing
floor and your wine press. Rejoice during your festival, you and
your sons and your daughters, your male and female slaves, as well
as the Levites, the strangers, the orphans, and the widows resident
in your town. (Deut. 16:13-14; see v. 11; 24:17-22; 26:12-13)

If the community neglects food for these least, it ceases to be Israel, rein-
vokes the practices of Pharaoh, and becomes a community monopoly that
breeds scarcity and violence.

2. The second text, as I read it, is an anti-text. That is, it is a report on
nonsharing. It is a report on the lavish royal table of King Solomon, who
lived a lush, shameless life:

Solomon's provision for one day was thirty cors of choice flour,
and sixty cors of meal, ten fat oxen, and twenty pasture-fed cattle,
one hundred sheep, besides deer, gazelles, roebucks, and fatted
fowl. (1 Kings 4:22-23)

In my judgment this text is ironic. It asserts that Israel and Judah "ate and
drank and were happy." It all sounds wonderful, rather like a government
report on the improving economy. It itemizes the wondrous extravagance of
the royal household. If you take only that in innocence, Solomon is indeed
wondrous. But we know better. We know that his rule ended in a civil war
about high taxes and what is called "forced labor," that is, the drafting into
state projects of those unable to buy their way out. What becomes clear in
reading the entire account of Solomon is that this lavish table of superflu-
ous food is at the expense of "the less fortunate" who, in their lack of
access, smolder and resent around the edges of society.

This is not a pretty picture of well-being. This is, in fact, a scenario in
which the few eat excessively at the expense of the many. Listen to the critique of Amos on such self-indulgence:

Alas for those who lie on beds of ivory,
and lounge on their couches,
and eat lambs from the flock,
and calves from the stall;
who sing idle songs to the sound of the harp,

and like David improvise on instruments of music;
who drink wine from bowls,
and anoint themselves with the finest oils,
but are not grieved over the ruin of Joseph. (Amos 6:4-6)

I cite Amos because the prophetic vision sees the end of Solomonic self-indulgence. The prophets see the destruction of society and a culmination in exile, deep social displacement. It requires no acute discernment to see that even as we speak, we are into a society of acute social displacement, precisely because of the Solomonic extravagance that stretches among us to obscene proportion. Unshared food, unshared long enough, leads to social displacement. The prophets saw it coming, but their contemporaries never got the point.

3. Later in Judaism, long after the deep displacement of exile, there is yet a third text on sharing. In this text, the community is arguing over punctiliousness about right worship. And into the dispute comes prophetic clarity. The poet has God say:

Is not this the fast that I choose:
to loose the bonds of injustice,
to undo the thongs of the yoke,
to let the oppressed go free,
and to break every yoke?
Is it not to share your bread with the hungry,
and bring the homeless poor into your house;
when you see the naked, to cover them,
and not to hide yourself from your own kin? (Isa. 58:6-7)

This is true religion, true obedience, true worship, true humanity. It is to undo the bonds of injustice that are deep and systemic. The alternative to oppression is sharing, not sharing as isolated acts of charity, but as public policy. The Bible is insistent that there is an alternative to the killing, monopolistic scarcity practiced by Pharaoh. It insists on:

- *departing* Pharaoh's system,
- *believing* in daily bread,
- *sharing* the bread across classes.

But observe, the triad of departing, believing, and sharing is to leave behind *the myth of scarcity* in order to embrace *the lyric of abundance*. That is our hope and our mandate.

VI

This move from God's creation *abundance* to Pharaoh's *monopoly and scarcity* to Israel's *ethic of sharing* is, of course, all in the Old Testament. But before I finish, I want to make a linkage to the New Testament and to the early church. Jesus came into a society tightly ordered by Roman governance and Jewish discipline. It was a society of skimpiness in religion, in law, and in economics. Into that uptightness Jesus uttered and enacted a remarkable alternative community. I will cite a series of texts that show Jesus doing and enacting bread-theology.

1. In the Sermon on the Mount, Jesus introduces a linkage between *anxiety* and *coveting* (see Luke 12:13-31). The thesis of his teaching is this:

> No one can serve two masters; for a slave will either hate the one
> and love the other, or be devoted to the one and despise the other.
> You cannot serve God and wealth. (Matt. 6:24)

It is instructive that the alternative to "God" is "wealth" (mammon, capital) that reflects hoarding in the face of scarcity. The God of the Bible is the complete antithesis to such fearful collecting. Jesus offers an alternative to the anxiety that assumes we never have enough:

> Therefore I tell you, do not worry about your life, what you will eat
> or what you will drink, or about your body, what you will wear.
> (Matt. 6:25)

The offer given is for some food, some drink, some clothing—all this is guaranteed. There is enough. No cause for worry, no cause for greed. As you know, the teaching concludes:

> But strive first for the kingdom of God and his righteousness, and
> all these things will be given to you as well. (Matt. 6:33)

"All these things" will be added; that is, food, clothing, well-being, all added when the community practices obedient neighborliness.

2. Jesus puts his life where his mouth was. What he said, he also did. In Mark 6:30-44, he came upon a crowd that was without bread and without a provider. He took the five loaves and two fish and then, we are told, "he took, he blessed, he broke, he gave." He performed a eucharistic act and the food multiplied. He made a sacramental gesture that acknowledged the holy dimension of creatureliness. Here there is nothing of anxiety, nothing of coveting, nothing of monopoly, nothing of scarcity, nothing of greed or hoarding. And the outcome is multiplying generosity. We are told there were five thousand people and twelve baskets of bread left over, an abundance that overrides all of the fearful anxiety of the world. Jesus is the impetus for ample bread for all of God's children.

3. The miracle of bread is replicated in Mark 8:1-9. The crowd is "without anything to eat." He has compassion. He has seven loaves. Again, "he took, he blessed, he broke, he gave." "They ate and were filled" (v. 8). There were four thousand folk there and there were seven baskets of bread left over. Jesus defies the wisdom of scarcity and summons the generosity of creation by his self-giving act of bread.

4. The feeding miracles of Mark are picked up in the Fourth Gospel (John 6:1-14). After the narrative of the miracle, the chapter offers an extended commentary. Jesus declared:

> I am the bread of life. Your ancestors ate the manna in the wilderness, and they died. This is the bread that comes down from heaven, so that one may eat of it and not die. I am the living bread that came down from heaven. Whoever eats of this bread will live forever; and the bread that I will give for the life of the world is my flesh. (vv. 48-51)

The "bread" now refers to the person of Jesus and life lived with him. The heavy christological accent would seem to move sharply away from the materiality of bread that concerns us here. Except that the Fourth Gospel stays close to the materiality of life. The offer of Jesus is that those who embrace him, his person and his mandate, will be deeply satisfied. Life in Christ fully overcomes the hunger of the world, including that primal hunger for bread. The Fourth Gospel shows how new and fresh is the power of Jesus to authorize a very different way in the world.

5. The miracle of bread evokes teaching about bread. Jesus is a master teacher. In Mark 8:14-21, the teacher moves from the known to the inscrutable. The narrative begins with a single telling note: They forget to bring any bread. People who forget to bring the bread are not paying attention. That means, of course, that they will eat somebody else's bread. And Jesus says:

> Watch out—beware of the yeast of the Pharisees and the yeast of Herod. (v. 15)

He might have said, beware of the bread of Pharaoh, because if you eat it, you will be back into the slavery of scarcity. And they answer, dummies that they are: "It is because we have no bread" (v. 16). And then he teaches:

> "Why are you talking about having no bread? Do you still not perceive or understand? Are your hearts hardened? Do you have eyes, and fail to see? Do you have ears, and fail to hear? . . . When I broke the five loaves for the five thousand, how many baskets full of broken pieces did you collect?" They said to him, "Twelve." "And the seven for the four thousand, how many baskets full of broken pieces did you collect?" And they said to him, "Seven." Then he said to them, "Do you not yet understand?" (Mark 8:17-21)

He reviews the lesson:

- When I fed five thousand: how many? Twelve.
- When I fed four thousand, how many? Seven.

And he said: "Do you not yet understand?" That is: You don't get it, do you? You do not get it about the bread. You do not understand that if you stay with the generous God, there is enough, there is more than enough, there is a surplus, everybody can eat. All have enough.

6. Do you know why they did not understand? There is added one isolated note in Mark 6:52 in the midst of all the bread talk:

> They did not understand about the loaves, but their hearts were hardened.

Hard hearts make bread-smarts impossible. "Hard hearts" refers back to hard-hearted Pharaoh. It means to live in a myth of scarcity with all the fearful anxiety that operates there, all the hoarding and brutality and monopoly. And if you live there, you will never understand about God's abundance.

So I end with a statement about God's abundance, in which we live. Christians know about God's abundance, and so we sing:

> Jesus calls us in, sends us out
> bearing fruit in a world of doubt,
> gives us love to tell, bread to share:
> God (Immanuel) everywhere!
> Jesus lives again,
> earth can breathe again,
> pass the Word around:
> *loaves abound!*[3]

Loaves abound! Twelve baskets, seven baskets, enough for all. Bread for the world, given out of God's generosity, because the people close to Jesus have departed Pharaoh and have learned to trust and know to share.

Jews have another word for it in Hebrew. It is *dayenu*. It means, there is enough in God's goodness. *Dayenu* is like "loaves abound." God overwhelms in generosity.

So we say: Loaves abound . . . *Dayenu!*

We sing, in the company of the creator God . . . *dayenu;*

> in the face of Pharaoh . . . *dayenu;*
> on the wilderness way . . . *dayenu;*
> into the good land of promise . . . *dayenu;*
> as we depart Pharaoh . . . *dayenu;*
> as we learn to trust heavenly bread . . . *dayenu;*
> as we share abundance . . . *dayenu;*
> as we stand in the crowd of five thousand . . . *dayenu;*
> as we eat with the four thousand . . . *dayenu;*
> as we leave scarcity for God's gifts . . . *dayenu;*
> as we face public policy questions . . . *dayenu;*
> as we pray daily for bread . . . *dayenu.*

That is what we sing: *dayenu, dayenu, dayenu.* And all the people said, *DAYENU!*

Abbreviations

BZAW	Beihefte zur ZAW
CBQ	*Catholic Biblical Quarterly*
HTR	*Harvard Theological Review*
JBL	*Journal of Biblical Literature*
JSNT	*Journal for the Study of the New Testament*
JSOT	*Journal for the Study of the Old Testament*
JSOTSup	Journal for the Study of the Old Testament—Supplement Series
NIB	*The New Interpreter's Bible*
OBT	Overtures to Biblical Theology
OTL	Old Testament Library
SBL	Society of Biblical Literature
SBLDS	SBL Dissertation Series
SBLMS	SBL Monograph Series
SBT	Studies in Biblical Theology
TBü	Theologische Bücherei
ZAW	*Zeitschrift für die alttestamentliche Wissenschaft*

Notes

Editor's Foreword

1. The other volumes are as follows: *Interpretation and Obedience: From Faithful Reading to Faithful Living* (Minneapolis: Fortress Press, 1991); *Old Testament Theology: Essays on Structure, Theme, and Text*, ed. Patrick D. Miller (Minneapolis: Fortress Press, 1992); *A Social Reading of the Old Testament: Prophetic Approaches to Israel's Communal Life*, ed. Patrick D. Miller (Minneapolis: Fortress Press, 1994); *The Psalms and the Life of Faith*, ed. Patrick D. Miller (Minneapolis: Fortress Press, 1995). In addition to these volumes, several previously published essays appeared in Brueggemann's *Cadences of Home: Preaching among Exiles* (Louisville: Westminster John Knox, 1997), and a collection of his sermons has been published with the title, *The Threat of Life: Sermons on Pain, Power, and Weakness*, ed. Charles L. Campbell (Minneapolis: Fortress Press, 1996).

2. For a sophisticated adaptation of the notion of "resonance" to an understanding of revelation and the theological task, see Claus Clausen, "Offenbarung als Resonanz," in *Resonanzen: Theologische Beiträge Michael Welker zum 50.Geburtstag*, ed. Sigrid Brandt and Bernd Oberdorfer (Wuppertal: Foedus-Verlag, 1997), 3–11.

3. Walter Brueggemann, *The Land* (OBT; Philadelphia: Fortress Press, 1977).

1. "Othering" with Grace and Courage

1. Hans Urs von Balthasar, *Theo-Drama: Theological Dramatic Theory I*, trans. G. Harrison (San Francisco: Ignatius Press, 1988) 626–27.

2. Emmanuel Levinas, *Totality and Infinity: An Essay on Exteriority* (Pittsburgh: Duquesne University Press, 1969), and *Otherwise Than Being* (Boston: Martinus Nijhoff, 1981) xxxi–iii and *passim*; George Steiner, *Real Presences* (Chicago: University of Chicago Press, 1989).

3. For representative statements, see D. W. Winnicott, *The Maturational Processes and the Facilitating Environment: Studies in the Theory of Emotional Development* (Madison, Conn.: International Universities Press, 1965), and *Playing & Reality* (London: Tavistock, 1971). See also Adam Phillips, *Winnicott* (Cambridge: Harvard University Press, 1988).

4. See for example, Winnicott, *The Maturational Processes*, 145–48.

5. On the "false self," see ibid., 140–52, and Phillips, *Winnicott, passim*.

6. Christopher Bollas, *The Shadow of the Object: Psychoanalysis of the Unthought Known* (New York: Columbia University Press, 1987) 137–40.

7. I suggest that in Psalm 39, the same double-bind is expressed toward God. In vv. 7-8 the speaker wants God's attention, but in v. 13 wants God to turn away. This entire psalm is an articulation of this dilemma.

8. Ana-Maria Rizzuto, *The Birth of the Living God: A Psychoanalytic Study* (Chicago: University of Chicago Press, 1979).

9. Ezek. 36:22-32 voices this odd reality. In that text, God does not express any caring for Israel, but only for God's own holy name. God can, however, only protect that holy name by concern for Israel, concern which is only a by-product of God's self-concern. See Walter Brueggemann, *Hopeful Imagination: Prophetic Voices in Exile* (Philadelphia: Fortress Press, 1986) 69–87.

10. On the dynamic and culmination of the canonical shape of the Psalms, see Walter Brueggemann, "Bounded by Obedience and Praise: The Psalms as Canon," *The Psalms and the Life of Faith,* ed. Patrick D. Miller (Minneapolis: Fortress, 1995) 189–213.

11. In Gen. 28:20-22, 32:26, Jacob is a model for urgent insistence on one's rights in the face even of God.

12. My phrasing, of course, means to refer to Martin Luther, "The Freedom of a Christian," *Three Treatises* (Philadelphia: Muhlenberg Press, 1960) 262–316.

13. Elizabeth O'Connor, *Our Many Selves: A Handbook for Self-Discovery* (New York: Harper & Row, 1971).

14. Roy Schafer, *Retelling a Life: Narration and Dialogue in Psychoanalysis* (New York: Basic Books, 1992) 21–35 and *passim.*

15. The reference calls to mind the infelicitous comment of Jimmy Carter, confessing that he had "sinned with his eyes."

16. Hans-Joachim Kraus, *Psalms 60-150: A Commentary,* trans. H. C. Oswald (Continental Commentaries; Minneapolis: Augsburg Books, 1989) 14. The Psalm translation is Kraus's.

17. Paul Ricoeur, "Fatherhood: From Phantasm to Symbol," *The Conflict of Interpretations,* ed. Don Ihde (Evanston, Ill.: Northwestern University Press, 1974) 468–97.

18. On these texts as baptismal texts, see Phillip Carrington, *The Primitive Christian Catechism: A Study in the Epistles* (Cambridge: Cambridge University Press, 1940).

2. The Daily Voice of Faith: The Covenanted Self

1. M. Douglas Meeks, *Origins of the Theology of Hope* (Philadelphia: Fortress Press, 1974) chapter 1 and *passim,* has provided a full exposition of Moltmann's understanding of the dialectic. See Jürgen Moltmann, *Theology of Hope: On the Ground and the Implications of a Christian Eschatology,* trans. J. W. Leitch (New York: Harper & Row, 1967) 211 and *passim,* and *The Crucified God: The Cross of Christ as the Foundation and Criticism*

of *Christian Theology*, trans. R. A. Wilson and J. Bowden (New York: Harper and Row, 1974) 27 and *passim*.

2. My use of the term "drama" is not without parallel to Reinhold Niebuhr, *The Self and the Dramas of History* (New York: Charles Scribner's Sons, 1955) 30–33, 84–85, 159.

3. Hans Urs von Balthasar, *Theo-Drama: Theological Dramatic Theory I*, trans. G. Harrison (San Francisco: Ignatius Press, 1988) 626–27.

4. Martin Buber, *I and Thou*, trans. R. G. Smith (New York: Charles Scribner's Sons, 1937).

5. Ferdinand Ebner, *Das Wort und die geistigen Realitaten: Pneumatologische Fragmente* (Innsbruck: Brenner, 1921). See also Shmuel Hugo Bergman, *Dialogical Philosophy from Kierkegaard to Buber* (Albany: SUNY Press, 1991) 155–61.

6. Emmanuel Levinas, *Totality and Infinity: An Essay on Exteriority* (Pittsburgh: Duquesne University Press, 1969), and *Otherwise Than Being or Beyond Essence* (Boston: Martinus Nijhoff, 1981) xxxi–xxxiii and *passim*. See also Robert Biggs, *Correlations in Rosenzweig and Levinas* (Princeton: Princeton University Press, 1992).

7. George Steiner, *Real Presences* (Chicago: University of Chicago Press, 1989).

8. See my comments above in "'Othering' with Grace and Courage," with particular reference to D. W. Winnicott. See also James W. Jones, *Contemporary Psychoanalysis and Religion: Transference and Transcendence* (New Haven, Conn.: Yale University Press, 1991), and Roy Schafer, *Retelling a Life: Narration and Dialogue in Psychoanalysis* (New York: Basic Books, 1992).

9. I know of no more powerful or lyrical assertion of God's Godness than by Alan Paton, "Meditation for a Young Boy Confirmed," *Knocking on the Door* (London: S.P.C.K., 1959) 89–90.

10. On the cruciality of obedience, see Abraham J. Heschel, *Who Is Man?* (Stanford: Stanford University Press, 1965) 111–12, and John Calvin, *Institutes of the Christian Religion I* (Library of Christian Classics 20; Philadelphia: Westminster Press, 1960) 72, who asserts, "All right knowledge of God is born of obedience."

11. Claus Westermann, "Zur Sammlung des Psalters," *Forschung am alten Testament* (TBü 24; Munich: Chr. Kaiser Verlag, 1964) 336–43, James Luther Mays, "The Place of the Torah-Psalms in the Psalter," *JBL* 106 (1987) 3–12, and "Psalm 118 in the Light of Canonical Analysis" in *Canon, Theology, and Old Testament Interpretation: Essays in Honor of Brevard S. Childs*, ed. by Gene M. Tucker et. al. (Philadelphia: Fortress Press, 1988) 299–311.

12. In addition to the articles of Mays in n. 11 above, see Gerald H. Wilson, "The Shape of the Book of Psalms," *Interpretation* 46 (1992) 129–42.

13. See the form-critical analysis of Claus Westermann, *The Structure of the Book of Job: A Form-Critical Analysis*, trans. C. A. Muenchow (Philadelphia:

Fortress Press, 1981).

14. This judgment, now well-established in scholarship, is deeply set against the older synthesis of Wellhausen who viewed "law" as only late and degenerative in Judaism. See Rolf Rendtorff, "The Image of Postexilic Israel in German Old Testament Scholarship from Wellhausen to von Rad," *Canon and Theology: Overtures to an Old Testament Theology* (OBT; Minneapolis: Fortress Press, 1993) 66–75.

15. See James Barr, *The Garden of Eden and the Hope of Immortality* (Minneapolis: Fortress Press, 1993) especially chapters 1 and 2.

16. See especially Krister Stendahl, "The Apostle Paul and the Introspective Conscience of the West," *HTR* 56 (1963) 199–215, now reprinted in *Paul Among Jews and Gentiles and Other Essays* (Philadelphia: Fortress Press, 1976) 78–96.

17. See Charles Taylor, *Sources of the Self: The Making of the Modern Identity* (Cambridge: Harvard University Press, 1989).

18. On the interplay of authority and autonomy see Richard Sennett, *Authority* (New York: Vintage Books, 1981).

19. See Philip Rieff, *The Triumph of the Therapeutic: Uses of Faith after Freud* (New York: Harper and Row, 1966), and more popularly, Robert Bellah et. al., *Habits of the Heart: Individualism and Commitment in American Life*, 2d ed. (Berkeley: University of California Press, 1996).

20. Adam Smith, *An Inquiry into the Nature and Causes of the Wealth of Nations*, ed. Edwin Cannan (Chicago: University of Chicago Press, 1976). I am grateful to Rupert Hoare for this important connection.

21. See Alice Miller, *Thou Shalt Not Be Aware: Society's Betrayal of the Child*, trans. H. Hannum and H. Hannum (New York: New American Library, 1991).

22. See Walter Brueggemann, *Finally Comes the Poet: Daring Speech for Proclamation* (Minneapolis: Fortress Press, 1989) 79–110, "The Commandments and Liberated, Liberating Bonding," *Interpretation and Obedience: From Faithful Reading to Faithful Living* (Minneapolis: Fortress Press, 1991) 145–58.

23. Norman K. Gottwald, *The Tribes of Yahweh: A Sociology of the Religion of Liberated Israel, 1250-1050 B.C.* (Maryknoll: Orbis Books, 1979) 93–99.

24. On the theological roots of Western political theory, see Charles S. McCoy and J. Wayne Baker, *Fountainhead of Federalism: Heinrich Bullinger and the Covenantal Tradition* (Louisville: Westminster/John Knox, 1991).

25. See Gottwald, *The Tribes of Yahweh*, 100–14.

26. See the summary and judgments of Ernest W. Nicholson, *God and His People: Covenant and Theology in the Old Testament* (Oxford: Clarendon Press, 1986).

27. Ben C. Ollenburger, *Zion the City of the Great King: A Theological Symbol of the Jerusalem Cult* (JSOTSup 41; Sheffield: Sheffield Academic

Press, 1987) makes a powerful case for the positive function of the temple symbolism in Israel. Yet on p. 159 he seems to concede that in practice much less may be claimed.

28. This sense of the dynamic of the text as Scripture is made clear in Gerald T. Sheppard, *The Future of the Bible: Beyond Liberalism and Literalism* (Toronto: United Church Publishing House, 1990) and his works cited there.

29. See Nils Peter Lemche, *The Canaanites and Their Land: The Tradition of the Canaanites* (JSOTSup 110; Sheffield: Sheffield Academic Press, 1991).

30. See Norbert Lohfink, "Distribution of the Functions of Power," *Great Themes from the Old Testament* (Edinburgh: T. & T. Clark, 1982) 55–75.

31. See Jon D. Levenson, *Creation and the Persistence of Evil: The Jewish Drama of Divine Omnipotence* (San Francisco: Harper and Row, 1988) 149–56.

32. It is important to recognize the scribal correction in v. 22, without which Abraham holds the initiative in the transaction.

33. On these and related texts, see Terence E. Fretheim, *The Suffering of God: An Old Testament Perspective* (OBT; Philadelphia: Fortress Press, 1984), and Samuel E. Balentine, *Prayer in the Hebrew Bible: The Drama of Divine-Human Dialogue* (OBT; Minneapolis: Fortress Press, 1993) 123–39.

34. See Sheldon H. Blank, "The Prophet as Paradigm," in *Essays in Old Testament Ethics,* ed. James L. Crenshaw and John T. Willis (New York: KTAV Publishing House, 1974) 111–30.

35. On the complaints of Jeremiah, see Kathleen M. O'Connor, *The Confessions of Jeremiah: Their Interpretation and Role in Chapters 1-25* (SBLDS 94; Atlanta: Scholars Press, 1988); A. R. Diamond, *The Confessions of Jeremiah in Context: Scenes of Prophetic Drama* (JSOT Sup 45; Sheffield: Sheffield Academic Press, 1987); and Mark S. Smith, *The Laments of Jeremiah and Their Contexts: A Literary and Redactional Study of Jeremiah 11-20* (SBLMS 42; Atlanta: Scholars Press, 1990).

36. Walter Baumgartner, *Jeremiah's Poems of Lament,* trans. D. E. Orton (Historic Texts and Interpreters in Biblical Scholarship; Decatur, Ga.: Almond Press, 1988).

37. See Westermann, *The Structure of the Book of Job,* 31-66.

38. The intent of 42:6 is enigmatic. Whether it functions as genuine submissiveness or mock submissiveness is much debated.

39. Christopher Bollas, *The Shadow of the Object: Psychoanalysis of the Unthought Known* (New York: Columbia University Press, 1987) 137–40.

40. See Norbert Lohfink, *The Covenant Never Revoked: Biblical Reflections on Christian-Jewish Dialogue,* trans. J. J. Scullion (New York: Paulist Press, 1991) 45–57 and *passim.*

41. Frederick Buechner, *Wishful Thinking: A Theological ABC* (New York: Harper and Row, 1973).

3. Duty as Delight and Desire: Preaching Obedience That Is Not Legalism

1. Paul R. McHugh, "Psychiatric Misadventures," *The Best American Essays 1993,* ed. Joseph Epstein (New York: Ticknor and Fields, 1993) 192, helpfully speaks of "cultural antinomianism" and explores its costliness for society. The best series of case studies for this condition is offered by Robert Bellah et. al., *Habits of the Heart: Individualism and Commitment in American Life,* 2d ed. (Berkeley: University of California Press, 1996).

2. Paul M. Van Buren, *A Theology of the Jewish-Christian Reality Part 2: A Christian Theology of the People Israel* (San Francisco: Harper & Row, 1987) 158–59 and *passim,* has explored a healthier understanding of the matter of Torah shared by Christians and Jews.

3. Krister Stendahl, "The Apostle Paul and the Introspective Conscience of the West," *Paul Among Jews and Gentiles and Other Essays* (Philadelphia: Fortress Press, 1976) 78–96.

4. Among his important works on the subject, see E. P. Sanders, *Paul and Palestinian Judaism: A Comparison of Patterns of Religion* (Philadelphia: Fortress Press, 1977). See his several discussions in the book on "covenantal nomism."

5. For a classic discussion of the issues of the Enlightenment vis-à-vis the traditional authority of the church, see Paul Hazard, *The European Mind 1680–1715* (New York: World Publishing Co., 1963).

6. On the production of conformity and homogeneity by the Enlightenment, see Colin Gunton, *Enlightenment & Alienation: An Essay Towards a Trinitarian Theology* (Grand Rapids. Eerdmans, 1985), and his more recent work, *The One, The Three, and The Many: God, Creation, and the Culture of Modernity* (Cambridge: Cambridge University Press, 1993).

7. Emil Fackenheim, *God's Presence in History* (New York: New York University Press, 1970) has shown how the dialectic of "saving and commanding" asserts the primal work of God with Israel.

8. The clearest, most direct statement of this tension is that of David Noel Freedman, "Divine Commitment and Human Obligation: The Covenant Theme," *Interpretation* 18 (1964) 419–31. Jon D. Levenson, *Sinai & Zion: An Entry into the Jewish Bible* (New York: Winston Press, 1985) has written a programmatic rebuttal of the antithesis commonly assumed in scholarship.

9. See the exposition of Brevard S. Childs, *Biblical Theology of the Old and New Testaments: Theological Reflection on the Christian Bible* (Minneapolis: Fortress Press, 1992) 532–65, and *Old Testament Theology in a Canonical Context* (Philadelphia: Fortress Press, 1985) 51–83.

10. Dennis H. Wrong, *The Problem of Order: What Unites and Divides Society* (New York: Free Press, 1994) 42–58, has written suggestively about the authority of expectation, though he is concerned for political theory and not theological force. He writes:

> The ambiguity of expectation becomes apparent only when we consider its use in communications such as that of a mother telling her child that she "expects" obedience at school to the teacher, or of the admiral addressing the fleet who affirms that "England expects every man to do his duty."
>
> The mother and the admiral are not simply predicting out loud future events or common interest. . . . Their utterances to the child and to the assembled fleet are in the imperative mode: the expectations asserted are intended to bring about the conduct they claim to be anticipating. . . . The child, after all, knows, and the mother knows the child knows, that disobedience at school will be reported at home and lead to possibly unpleasant results. . . .
>
> Expectations may, I have argued, function as imperatives, as normative demands constraining the human objects of expectation to conform to them. . . . The emergence of expectations-cum-norms out of recurrent interaction is a process that goes on all the time, if often in trivial and evanescent ways. (42–43, 46, 51)

11. Notice that often the "sanction" is not articulated but is inherent in the expectation itself, because of the authority of the one who expects.

12. This seems to be recognized even in popular ways, so that the attempt at "unconditional" finally requires some conditionality. See the belated discovery of this in William H. Masters and Virginia E. Johnson, *The Pleasure Bond: A New Look at Sexuality and Commitment* (Boston: Little, Brown, 1974), and the analysis of Daniel Yankelovitch, *New Rules: Searching for Self-Fulfillment in a World Turned Upside Down* (New York: Bantam Books, 1982).

13. This is a point at which Karl Barth's resistance of the *analogia entis* and his embrace of *analogia fidei* might be considered. Eberhard Busch, *Karl Barth: His Life from Letters and Autobiographical Texts,* trans. J. Bowden (Philadelphia: Fortress Press, 1976) 215–16 and *passim*, places Barth's concerns in context.

14. E. Kutsch, "Gesetz und Gnade. Probleme des alttestamentlichen Bundesbegriffs," *ZAW* 79 (1967) 18–35, goes so far as to suggest that "covenant" (*berîth*) in fact means "obligation."

15. George E. Mendenhall, *Law and Covenant in Israel and the Ancient Near East* (Pittsburgh: The Biblical Colloquium, 1955) made the case that "sanctions" belong to the structure and substance of covenant. More generally, see the discussion of Wrong (n. 10) on the reality of sanctions in social relations.

16. "Covenantal nomism" (on which see Sanders, n. 4) nicely juxtaposes terms which articulate the subtle dimensions of covenant as a *relation* and as a *demand*.

17. On this phrase, see the old but reliable discussion of Walther Eichrodt, "The Holy One in Your Midst: The Theology of Hosea," *Interpretation* 15 (1961) 259–73.

18. On "the way" as a governing image for Israel's life of obedient faith, see James Muilenburg, *The Way of Israel: Biblical Faith and Ethics* (New York: Harper & Brothers, 1961) and Paul van Buren, *Discerning the Way: A Theology of the Jewish-Christian Reality* (New York: Seabury Press, 1980).

19. Concerning the ambiguity and complexity of the commandments which require ongoing interpretation, see Walter Brueggemann "The Commandments and Liberated, Liberating Bonding," *Interpretation and Obedience: From Faithful Reading to Faithful Living* (Minneapolis: Fortress Press, 1991) 145–58.

20. I understand legalism to refer to commands which are imposed but not gladly received and embraced as one's own. The model of Job's friends is the standard example in the Bible. Such imposition tends to be rigid and coercive, without taking into account the impact of context or experience. On this matter as it relates to freedom and health, see Christopher Bollas, *The Shadow of the Object: Psychoanalysis of the Unthought Known* (New York: Columbia University Press, 1987) 135–156, and his notion of a "normotic personality."

21. More than anyone else, Norman K. Gottwald, *The Tribes of Yahweh: A Sociology of the Religion of Liberated Israel, 1250–1050 B.C.* (Maryknoll: Orbis Books, 1979) 489–92 and *passim*, has shown the ways in which Israel is revolutionary in terms of its social intention. Gottwald's articulation is enormously valuable, even if one does not follow all of his socio-historical analysis.

22. On the relationship between baptism and preaching, see William H. Willimon, *Peculiar Speech· Preaching to the Baptized* (Grand Rapids: Eerdmans, 1992).

23. It will be recognized that my approach here flies in the face of the classic arguments of Anders Nygren, *Agape and Eros* (Philadelphia: Westminster Press, 1932, 1938, 1939, 1953). I do this with considerable diffidence, because I am thoroughly schooled in Nygren's argument. I have come to think, however, that Nygren imposed categories that may have been required in his context, but that in doing so, he overlooked dimensions of the ethic of Israel and the church that moved beyond duty to the embrace of joy in faith. For our purposes, Nygren's discussion of Augustine (449-563) is especially important. I should also mention that William Moran, "The Ancient Near Eastern Background of the Love of God in Deuteronomy," *CBQ* 25 (1963) 77–87, has shown that in some cases in the ancient Near East, "love" is a political word bespeaking acknowledgment of sovereignty.

24. John Calvin, *Commentary on the Book of Psalms, Volume Second* (Grand Rapids: Baker Book House, 1979) 155. It should be noted, however, that Calvin still resists the notion of the intrinsic satisfaction of the rela-

tionship, and must appeal to "the plentitude of blessing" that seems extrinsic to the relation of communion itself.

25. Augustine, *The Confessions of St. Augustine, Bishop of Hippo* (New York: E. P. Dutton, 1951) 1.

26. Ibid., 5. Special attention should be given to the recent study of the *Confessions* by Margaret R. Miles, *Desire and Delight: A New Reading of Augustine's Confessions* (New York: Crossroad, 1992). Against the grain of the argument of Nygren, Miles proposes that the *Confessions* are intended by Augustine to be a "text of pleasure," and that the pleasure of the reader is linked to Augustine's own struggle for pleasure. His argument is that he tried every pleasure the world could offer and only finds his true desire in communion with God. This is not a stifling of desire but the proper focus on the desire which is appropriate to the human heart. Miles summarizes her argument:

> The *Confessions* is, among other things, a narrative deconstruction of what is ordinarily thought of as pleasurable, and a reconstruction of "true" pleasure. . . . He was quite clear about what constituted the condition of greatest pleasure by the time he wrote the *Confessions*. . . . The pleasure experiment has come to a dead end. . . . The key to pleasure, for Augustine, was ideally not the sacrifice of some pleasures so that others could be cultivated. It was the ordering of all the pleasures of a human life so that those associated with enjoyment of objects in the sensible world would not usurp all of a person's attention and affection. When pleasures are constellated around a single object of love, he said, they can be enjoyed without fear of distraction. . . . Augustine learned more than he acknowledged from sex, that he learned "the deep and irreplaceable knowledge of [his] capacity for joy" from his sexual experience, and that it was precisely this experimental knowledge from which Augustine extrapolated his model of spiritual pleasure.(20, 32, 37, 71)

27. On the decalogue, see Walter Harrelson, *The Ten Commandments and Human Rights* (OBT; Philadelphia: Fortress Press, 1980), and Brevard S. Childs, *Old Testament Theology*, 63–83.

28. This is, of course, reminiscent of the classic answer of the Westminster Catechism, "Man's Chief End is to glorify God and enjoy him forever." It is striking that the second half of the sentence speaks of the "enjoyment of God," which is the satisfaction of desire that encompasses duty and moves beyond duty to delight.

29. A proviso is important that such a notion is not an invitation for the preacher to focus on his or her favorite causes or animosities. My impression is that rightly done, the notion of critical obedience gives aid and comfort to no one, but challenges all of our pet modes of utilitarian obedience.

30. On this theme, see Gerhard von Rad, "Brother and Neighbor in the Old Testament," in *God at Work in Israel*, trans. J. H. Marks (Nashville: Abingdon Press, 1980) 183–93.

31. Marva J. Dawn, *Sexual Character: Beyond Technique to Intimacy* (Grand Rapids: Eerdmans, 1993) has shown in a fine study how a rather conventional sexual ethic is open to a much more dense significance.

32. It cannot be said too often, that after Israel (or we) arrive at workable rules, the rules endlessly require ongoing interpretation to take account of context, experience, and new learning. This is inevitable, and we either do it knowingly or without recognizing that we are doing such interpretation.

33. See the thoughtful discussion of the issues by Ulrich Duchrow, *Global Economy: A Confessional Issue for the Churches?* (Geneva: WCC Publications, 1987).

34. John Kenneth Galbraith, *The Culture of Contentment* (Boston: Houghton Mifflin, 1992), has written an acute study of this propensity in enclaves of wealth in our society.

35. Marvin L. Chaney, "You Shall Not Covet Your Neighbor's House," *Pacific Theological Review* 15 (Winter, 1982) 3–13, has shown how the tenth commandment is concerned with policies and practices of systemic acquisitiveness.

36. A classic example of this incongruity is the way in which Roman Catholics in this country are uncompromisingly zealous about the issue of abortion (and other matters of sexuality), but are largely indifferent to the wondrous Bishops' Letter on economics. Roman Catholics are no more caught in this than other Christians. I cite the example only because the pastoral letters of the bishops would make possible a discussion of both issues, but that discussion is almost everywhere resisted.

37. This contradiction especially sends mixed messages to children and young people. As the commoditization of all of life is encouraged, it is difficult then to imagine that sexuality is an exception to the general rule of promiscuity on which our consumer society is dependent.

38. Martin Buber, *Tales of the Hasadim: The Early Masters*, trans. O. Marx (London: Thames and Hudson, 1956) 212, cites such a prayer from the rabbi of Berditchev:

> Where I wander—You!
> Where I ponder—You!
> Only you, You again, always You!
> You! You! You!
> When I am gladdened—You!
> When I am saddened—You!
> Only You, You again, always You!
> You! You! You!

39. It is worth noticing that the term "desired" is *ḥamad*, the same word that is rendered "covet" in the commandment. Israel properly covets, that is, desires the commandments, the same desiring done by the couple in the garden in Genesis. Israel is supposed to "desire." It matters decisively *what* Israel desires.

4. Justice: The Earthly Form of God's Holiness

1. On the antecedents, see David Noel Freedman and David Frank Graf, eds., *Palestine in Transition: The Emergence of Ancient Israel* (The Social World of Biblical Antiquity Series 2; Sheffield: Almond Press, 1983), and recently and popularly, Hershel Shanks et al., *The Rise of Ancient Israel* (Washington: Biblical Archaeology Society, 1992).

2. Sandra M. Schneiders, *The Revelatory Text: Interpreting the New Testament as Sacred Scripture* (San Francisco: Harper, 1991) 102–8, uses the happy parallel term "Paschal Imagination."

3. The phrase, of course, refers to the program of Karl Marx. On his insistence upon the emancipation of human persons from fate, see Karl Marx, *Early Writings,* trans. R. Livingston and G. Benton (New York: Penguin Books, 1975) 379–400, and José P. Miranda, *Marx Against the Marxists,* trans. J. Drury (Maryknoll: Orbis Books, 1980) 29–68 and *passim.*

4. On my understanding of the plot, see Walter Brueggemann, *Hope within History* (Atlanta: John Knox Press, 1987) 7–26.

5. My friend Tom Green has helped me see that even the word "justice" as used in the Old Testament is likely to be misunderstood in contemporary usage because of the radically different notion of justice in ancient Israel and ancient Greece. Our Greek understandings render the Israelite usage most difficult.

6. Michael Walzer, *Exodus and Revolution* (New York: Basic Books, 1985).

7. The case has been most rigorously made by Norman K. Gottwald, *The Tribes of Yahweh: A Sociology of the Religion of Liberated Israel, 1250–1050 B.C.* (Maryknoll: Orbis Books, 1979). See his more recent articulation of the hypothesis with changed terminology, "Responses," in Hershel Shanks et al., *The Rise of Ancient Israel* (Washington: Biblical Archaeology Society, 1992) 70–75.

8. The best recent summary of scholarship on the Ten Commandments is by Walter Harrelson, *The Ten Commandments and Human Rights* (OBT; Philadelphia: Fortress Press, 1980). On the commandments and nihilism, Cynthia Ozick, "Round Table Discussion," *Writing and the Holocaust,* ed. Berel Lang (New York: Holmes and Meier, 1988) 280, has written:

> Another way of reflection on the why is to note that the Jews vis-à-vis nihilism, stand for No: not the No of nihilism, but the No against nihilism, the No that presses for restraint. . . . If you listen to the Commandments in Hebrew, you will hear a no-nonsense abruptness, a rapidity and a terseness. They begin with Lo, the Hebrew word for No. Lo tignov, Do not steal. Punkt. The Torah the Jews carry stands for No, for all the things we ordinary mortals want to do and take glee in doing. The Jews stand for the hard demands of monotheism—nobody wants monotheism . . . the burden of being the people that carries monotheism into the world, monotheism with its uncompromising obligations to mercy, monotheism with its invention of conscience.

9. On the relationship of idolatry and ideology, see Walter Brueggemann, *Israel's Praise: Doxology Against Idolatry and Ideology* (Philadelphia: Fortress Press, 1988).

10. See especially Patrick D. Miller, "The Human Sabbath: A Study in Deuteronomic Theology," *Princeton Theological Seminary Bulletin* 6 (1985) 81-97, and *Deuteronomy* (Interpretation; Louisville: John Knox Press, 1990) 79-84. Miller, *Deuteronomy*, 83, refers to the sabbath commandment as "a primary impetus to social justice." Marva J. Dawn, *Keeping the Sabbath Wholly: Ceasing, Resting, Embracing, Feasting* (Grand Rapids: Eerdmans, 1989) has poignantly voiced the contemporary urgency of the sabbath.

11. Visions of this community are evident in the sufficiency of manna in Exod. 16:17-18, and in the vision of reconciled creation in Isa. 11:6-9.

12. See Walter Brueggemann, *Finally Comes the Poet: Daring Speech for Proclamation* (Minneapolis: Fortress Press, 1989) 79–110, and *Interpretation and Obedience* (Minneapolis: Fortress Press, 1991) 145–58.

13. For a conventional, reliable introduction to this corpus, see Dale Patrick, *Old Testament Law* (Atlanta: John Knox Press, 1985).

14. Paul D. Hanson, "The Theological Significance of Contradiction within the Book of the Covenant," in *Canon and Authority: Essays in Old Testament Religion and Theology*, ed. G. W. Coats and B. O. Long (Philadelphia: Fortress Press, 1977) 110–31, has shown the contradictions within the corpus. It is not necessary, however, to conclude with Hanson that the two attitudes need to be, or even can be, divided into separate and distinct sources. The fact that they come together discloses more poignantly the character of Israel's problematic thinking about its social vision.

15. Jeffries M. Hamilton, *Social Justice and Deuteronomy: The Case of Deuteronomy 15* (SBLDS 136; Atlanta: Scholars Press, 1992).

16. On the relation of the economy to the larger social fabric, see Karl Polanyi, *The Great Transformation* (Boston: Beacon Press, 1957), and the theological use made of his argument by M. Douglas Meeks, *God the Economist: The Doctrine of God and Political Economy* (Minneapolis: Fortress Press, 1989).

17. Norbert Lohfink, "Distribution of the Functions of Power," *Great Themes from the Old Testament* (Edinburgh: T. & T. Clark, 1982) 55–75.

18. In addition to Lohfink, see S. Dean McBride, "Polity of the Covenant People: The Book of Deuteronomy," *Interpretation* 41 (1987) 229–44.

19. For a theological understanding of this problem, see Walther Zimmerli, *The Law and the Prophets: A Study of the Meaning of the Old Testament*, trans. R. E. Clements (New York: Harper and Row, 1963). Most recently see Brian Peckham, *History and Prophecy: The Development of Late Judean Literary Traditions* (New York: Doubleday, 1993).

20. See Ronald Clements, "Patterns in the Prophetic Canon," in *Canon and Authority*, 42–55.

21. For the term "metahistory," see Klaus Koch, *The Prophets Vol. I: The Assyrian Period*, trans. M. Kohl (Philadelphia: Fortress Press, 1982) 144 and *passim*. Koch also uses the term "suprahistory."

22. On Amos, see James Luther Mays, "Justice: Perspectives from the Prophetic Tradition," *Interpretation* 37 (1983) 5–17, and more generally Bernhard Lang, "The Social Organisation of Peasant Poverty in Biblical Israel," *JSOT* 24 (1982) 47–63. Mays and Lang speak variously of "early capitalism" and "rent capitalism."

23. On this text, see José P. Miranda, *Marx and the Bible: A Critique of the Philosophy of Oppression*, trans. J. Eagleson (Maryknoll: Orbis Books, 1974) 47–62.

24. On the sociological aspects of prophecy, see Robert R. Wilson, *Prophecy and Society in Ancient Israel* (Philadelphia: Fortress Press, 1980).

25. The messenger formula "Thus saith the Lord" is a claim of "metahistorical" authority for prophetic utterance which intends to counter other presumed authorities in the conversation.

26. On the cruciality of justice in the faith of the Psalter, see J. David Pleins, *The Psalms: Songs of Tragedy, Hope, and Justice* (Maryknoll: Orbis Books, 1993), and Walter Brueggemann, *The Message of the Psalms: A Theological Commentary* (Minneapolis: Augsburg, 1984) 168–76.

27. On this verse and its focus on justice, see the comment of Hans-Joachim Kraus, *Psalms 60-150*, trans. H. C. Oswald (Continental Commentaries; Minneapolis: Augsburg Books, 1989) 270.

28. Gerald T. Sheppard, "'Enemies' and the Politics of Prayer in the Book of Psalms," in *The Bible and Liberation: Political and Social Hermeneutics*, ed. N. K. Gottwald and R. A. Horsley (Maryknoll: Orbis Books, 1993) 376–91, and "Theology and the Book of Psalms," *Interpretation* 46 (1992) 143-55, has suggested that the imperatives of the psalms are voiced so that the oppressors may "overhear" and are in fact addressed to them. I do not see that it is necessary to make the matter an either/or. The prayers may be both "real address" and "overhearing."

29. Verses 3-4 are not addressed as imperatives to Yahweh, but appear to be imperatives addressed by Yahweh to the other would-be gods. In any case, the subject matter is telling and points to v. 9.

30. The juxtaposition of the two, human conduct and Yahweh's own work, is nicely visible in the juxtaposition of Pss. 111 and 112, which in turn affirm the justice of Yahweh and the justice of God's righteous people.

31. See James L. Mays, "The Place of the Torah-Psalms," *JBL* 106 (1987) 3–13, and J. Clinton McCann Jr., *A Theological Introduction to the Book of Psalms: The Psalms as Torah* (Nashville: Abingdon Press, 1993) 25–40 and *passim*.

32. On this tension, see Leo G. Perdue, "Cosmology and the Social Order in the Wisdom Tradition," in *The Sage in Israel and the Ancient Near East*, ed. J. G. Gammie and L. G. Perdue (Winona Lake: Eisenbrauns, 1990) 457–78.

33. On the social location of wisdom, see the early and compelling proposal of Robert Gordis, "The Social Background of Wisdom Literature," *Poets, Prophets, and Sages: Essays in Biblical Interpretation* (Bloomington: Indiana University Press, 1971) 160–97, and the more recent, more complex scholarly judgments in the collection, *The Sage in Israel,* ed. Gammie and Perdue. On the matter of "wealth and poverty," see for example, J. David Pleins, "Poverty in the Social World of the Wise," *JSOT* 37 (1987) 61–78, and R. N. Whybray, *Wealth and Poverty in the Book of Proverbs* (JSOTSup 99; Sheffield: JSOT Press, 1990).

34. On the voice of the friends as a theological stance, see Claus Westermann, *The Structure of the Books of Job: A Form-Critical Analysis,* trans. C. A. Muenchow (Philadelphia: Fortress Press, 1981) 81–95; Gustavo Gutiérrez, *On Job: God-Talk and the Suffering of the Innocent,* trans. M. J. O'Connell (Maryknoll: Orbis Books, 1987) 21–38; and, more broadly, David J. A. Clines, "Deconstructing the Book of Job," *What Does Eve Do to Help?* (JSOTSup 94; Sheffield: JSOT Press 1990) 106–23.

5. The Cunning Little Secret of Certitude: On the First Great Commandment

1. Abraham Heschel, *Who Is Man?* (Stanford: Stanford University Press, 1965) 97–98.

2. John Calvin, *Institutes of the Christian Religion* I (The Library of Christian Classics 20; Philadelphia: Westminster Press, 1960) 72.

3. Cynthia Ozick, "Roundtable Discussion," in *Writing and the Holocaust,* ed. Berel Lang (New York: Holmes and Meier, 1988) 280.

6. Neighborliness and the Limits of Power in God's Realm: On the Second Great Commandment

1. Cynthia Ozick, "Roundtable Discussions," in *Writing and the Holocaust,* ed. Berel Lang (New York: Holmes and Meier, 1988) 280.

2. Jeffries M. Hamilton, *Social Justice & Deuteronomy: The Case of Deuteronomy 15* (SBLDS 136; Atlanta: Scholars Press, 1992), and Moshe Weinfeld, *Social Justice in Ancient Israel and in the Ancient Near East* (Minneapolis: Fortress Press, 1995).

3. Patrick D. Miller, *Deuteronomy* (Interpretation; Louisville: Westminster/John Knox Press, 1990) 134–40, and "The Human Sabbath: A Study in Deuteronomic Theology," *Princeton Theological Seminary Bulletin* 6 (1985) 81–97.

4. Patrick D. Miller, "Luke 4:16-21," *Interpretation* 29 (1975) 417–21.

5. Raimon Panikkar, *Cultural Disarmament: The Way to Peace,* trans. R. R. Barr (Louisville: Westminster/John Knox Press, 1995) 62.

6. The speech is excerpted in Gerald Gunther, *Learned Hand: The Man and the Judge* (New York: Alfred A. Knopf, 1994) 549.

7. Truth-Telling as Subversive Obedience

1. For a parallel consideration of the fourth and tenth commandments, see Walter Brueggemann, *Finally Comes the Poet: Daring Speech for Proclamation* (Minneapolis: Fortress Press, 1989) 79–110, and "The Commandments and Liberated, Liberating Bonding," in *Interpretation and Obedience: From Faithful Reading to Faithful Living* (Minneapolis: Fortress Press, 1991) 145–58.

2. The literature on the decalogue is immense. In addition to the magisterial and normative interpretations of Luther and Calvin, see Walter Harrelson, *The Ten Commandments and Human Rights* (OBT; Philadelphia: Fortress Press, 1980); Brevard S. Childs, *Old Testament Theology in a Canonical Context* (Philadelphia: Fortress Press, 1985) 63–83; Paul Lehmann, *The Decalogue and a Human Future: The Meaning of the Commandments for Making and Keeping Human Life Human* (Grand Rapids: Eerdmans, 1994); and Horst Dietrich Preuss, *Old Testament Theology I* (OTL; Louisville: Westminster John Knox Press, 1995) 100–17.

3. A range of texts are related to this commandment and some perhaps derived from it: Exod. 23:1; 6-8; Lev. 19:11, 16-17; Deut. 19:15ff.; Amos 2:7; 5:15; Mic. 3:11; Pss. 12:2; 27:2; 64:8; Prov. 11:9-13.

4. There is a long-standing critical tradition that situates the judicial provisions of Exodus 18 in the context of Jehoshaphat's reform, on which see 2 Chron. 19:4-11. While such a critical judgment may be made, the text as it stands makes a claim for Mosaic authorization.

5. See Thomas W. Overholt, *The Threat of Falsehood: A Study in the Theology of the Book of Jeremiah* (SBT 2/16; London: SCM Press, 1970).

6. The issue of false and true prophecy is enormously vexed. While it may be claimed that there is nothing that *formally* distinguishes false and true prophets, it is clear that *in substance* ancient Israel, in its canonizing process, made important distinctions. For representative views of the issue, see James L. Crenshaw, *Prophetic Conflict: Its Effect upon Israelite Religion* (BZAW 124; Berlin: de Gruyter, 1971), and James A. Sanders, "Canonical Hermeneutics: True and False Prophecy," in *From Sacred Story to Sacred Text* (Philadelphia: Fortress Press, 1987) 87–105. On the classic case of Jeremiah 27–28, see Henri Mottu, "Jeremiah vs. Hananiah: Ideology and Truth in Old Testament Prophecy," in *The Bible and Liberation: Political and Social Hermeneutics,* ed. N. K. Gottwald (Maryknoll: Orbis Books, 1983) 235–51.

7. The NRSV renders the first word "Ah." That innocuous translation is unfortunate, for the term bespeaks sadness at loss and death. The word indicates a sense of loss that is to come on those who practice deceiving euphemism.

8. Robert J. Lifton, *The Nazi Doctors: Medical Killing and the Psychology of Genocide* (New York: Basic Books, 1986) 202 and *passim*.

9. Chomsky's argument in this regard is stated in many places. See for example, *Necessary Illusions: Thought Control in Democratic Societies*

(Boston: South End Press, 1989); *What Uncle Sam Really Wants* (Tucson: Odonian Press, 1992); and *The Washington Connection and Third World Fascism* (Boston: South End Press, 1979). My own references are from a lecture he presented in June, 1995.

10. See especially Neil Postman, *Amusing Ourselves to Death: Public Discourse in the Age of Show Business* (New York: Penguin Books, 1986), *Technopoly: The Surrender of Culture to Technology* (New York: Random House, 1993), and *How to Watch TV News* (New York: Viking Penguin, 1992).

11. The most important studies of the theme are by Jacques Ellul, *The Humiliation of the Word*, trans. J. M. Hanks (Grand Rapids: Eerdmans, 1991); *Propaganda: The Formation of Men's Attitudes,* trans. K. Kellen and J. Lerner (New York: Random House, 1973); and *Technological Society,* trans. J. Wilkinson (New York: Random House, 1967).

12. Karl Marx has seen this with the greatest clarity and influence. Note his programmatic statement: The criticism of heaven is thus transformed into the criticism of earth, the criticism of religion into the criticism of law, and the criticism of theology into the criticism of politics. See David McLellan, *The Thought of Karl Marx: An Introduction* (London: Macmillan Press, 1971) 22.

13. On the importance of juridical language in the Fourth Gospel, see Robert V. Moss, "The Witnessing Church in the New Testament," *Theology and Life 3* (1960) 262–68; Andrew T. Lincoln, "Trials, Plots and the Narrative of the Fourth Gospel," *JSNT 56* (1994) 3–30; and more generally A. A. Trites, *The New Testament Concept of Witness* (Cambridge: Cambridge University Press, 1977) 78–127. Most remarkably, the Fourth Gospel affirms the Paraclete as a witness to Jesus, on which see Gail R. O'Day, "Excursus: The Paraclete," and "The Gospel of John: Introduction, Commentary, and Reflections," *NIB* 9 (1995) 774–78.

14. On this text, see the helpful comments of O'Day, ibid., 815–27, and the shrewd interpretation by Paul Lehmann, *The Transfiguration of Politics* (New York: Harper and Row, 1975) 48–70.

15. See M. Scott Peck, *People of the Lie: The Hope for Healing Human Evil* (New York: Simon and Schuster, 1985).

16. Richard N. Goodwin, "A Three-Party Election Won't Address Issue of Economic Injustice," *Boston Globe* (Friday, July 26, 1996) A17.

8. "Placed" between Promise and Command

1. See Niels Peter Lemche, *The Canaanites and Their Land: The Tradition of the Canaanites* (JSOTSup 110; Sheffield: JSOT Press, 1991).

2. See Jeffries M. Hamilton, *Social Justice and Deuteronomy: The Case of Deuteronomy 15* (SBLDS 136; Atlanta: Scholars Press, 1992).

3. See Norbert Lohfink, "Distribution of the Functions of Power," *Great Themes from the Old Testament* (Edinburgh: T. & T. Clark, 1982) 55–75.

9. The Truth of Abundance: Relearning Dayenu

1. M. Douglas Meeks, *God the Economist: The Doctrine of God and Political Economy* (Minneapolis: Fortress Press, 1989), and Regina M. Schwartz, *The Curse of Cain: The Violent Legacy of Monotheism* (Chicago: University of Chicago Press, 1997).

2. See, for example, Charles Reich, *Opposing the System* (New York: Random House, 1995).

3. Fred Koan, "Let Us Talents and Tongues Employ."

Credits

"'Othering' with Grace and Courage" was originally published in *The Anglican* (Fall/Winter 1993–94).

"The Daily Voice of Faith: The Covenanted Self" was originally published in *Sewanee Theological Review* 37:2 (Easter 1994), published quarterly by the School of Theology of the University of the South, Sewanee, Tennessee.

"Duty as Delight and Desire: Preaching Obedience That Is Not Legalism" was originally published in *Journal for Preachers* 18:1 (Advent 1994). Copyright © 1994 *Journal for Preachers*, P.O. Box 520, Decatur, GA 30031.

"Justice: The Earthly Form of God's Holiness" was originally published in *Reformed World* (March 1994). Copyright © 1994 World Alliance of Reformed Churches, Geneva.

"The Cunning Little Secret of Certitude: On the First Great Commandment" and "Neighborliness and the Limits of Power in God's Realm: On the Second Great Commandment" were originally published in *Church and Society* (July/August 1997).

"Truth-Telling as Subversive Obedience" was originally published in *Journal for Preachers* 20:2 (Lent 1997). Copyright © 1997 *Journal for Preachers*, P.O. Box 520, Decatur, GA 30031.

"'Placed' between Promise and Command" was originally published in *Rooted in the Land: Essays on Community and Place*, ed. W. Vitek and W. Jackson (New Haven: Yale University Press, 1996) 124–31. Copyright © 1996 Yale University Press.

Scripture Index